talking to "crazy"

How to Deal with the
Irrational and Impossible
People in Your Life

MARK GOULSTON

HARPERCOLLINS
LEADERSHIP

AN IMPRINT OF HARPERCOLLINS

Library of Congress Cataloging-in-Publication Data

Names: Goulston, Mark, author.
Title: Talking to crazy : how to deal with the irrational and impossible people in your life / Mark Goulston.
Description: New York, NY : AMACOM, a division of American Management Association, [2018] I Includes index.
Identifiers: LCCN 2018001753 (print) I LCCN 2018013512 (ebook) I ISBN 9780814439593 (ebook) I ISBN 9780814439296 (pbk.)
Subjects: LCSH: Interpersonal conflict. I Interpersonal relations. I Conflict management.
Classification: LCC BF637.I48 (ebook) I LCC BF637.I48 G68 2018 (print) I DDC 158.2--dc23
LC record available at https://lccn.loc.gov/2018001753

Published by HarperCollins Leadership, an imprint of HarperCollins.

Printed in the United States of America

HB 10.12.2021

Dedication

To the loving memory of Warren Bennis, whose greatest gift to me was making it clear within five minutes of meeting him that I could trust him to never hurt me—a quality I do my best to aspire to and emulate.

Contents

**SECTION 5 What to Do When
Crazy Is Actually Mental Illness / 211**

Acknowledgments

Writing a book is a crazy-making process, and I want to thank the people who kept me sane while I put my ideas on the page. I'm especially grateful to my editor at AMACOM, Ellen Kadin, who juggles the dual roles of good friend and tough critic with immense skill and grace. I also appreciate the contributions of Erika Spelman and Louis Greenstein, who helped me shape a rough work into the book you're reading. And many, many thanks to Bill Gladstone and Margot Maley Hutchison at Waterside Productions, both agents extraordinaire.

Many other people deserve a thank-you for supporting me throughout the writing process and contributing ideas and suggestions that made the book better. They include Irene Majuk, Rosemary Carlough, Susan Zeidman, Nancy Roberson, Alison Blake, Kama Timbrell, Keith Ferrazzi, Seth Godin, Colonel Tom Tyrrell, General Marty Steele, Xavier Amador, Pete Linnett, Mimi Grant, Bob Kelley, David Feinberg, Jim Mazzo, Bill Liao, David Wurth, Ken Rutkowski, and Jason Dean.

Special thanks to Marshall Goldsmith for favoring me with his wonderful Foreword, Bruce Heller, my partner at the Goulston Group, and Clark Vautier, my manager. Their continued enthusiasm for this book and my ideas continue to inspire me every day.

Above all, I thank my wife, Lisa; my children Billy, Lauren, Emily, and son-in-law Pete D'Agostino for their unending love, tolerance, and patience; and my brothers, Noel Goulston and Robert Goulston, and their wives and children, for their constant support —through all the sane and the crazy.

Foreword

When you ask people in the workplace, "What is a greater cause of stress, too much work or difficult people?", nearly three to one will answer that it is difficult people. My entire coaching career has been focused on helping high-achieving people become even more successful by eliminating those specific behaviors that make *them* difficult to deal with. But what do you do if you are on the *receiving* end of such behavior?

Lucky for me, I've rarely had problems with such people. In fact, anyone who knows me, or with whom I've corresponded by email, knows that I end my communications with "Life is good." That's because, as a Buddhist, I generally believe that to be true. Another reason is that irrational and impossible people don't generally get the better of me. If people who ought to change don't want to change, that's their choice; but such people *don't* drive me crazy, because it is *my* choice not to work with or deal with them.

That said, of course I realize that many people—in fact most people—are not so fortunate as to be able to choose with whom they deal both in their day-to-day work lives and with their families and friends.

I have often wished for a guide to offer my own friends to help them better deal with those people who continue to drive them crazy, so they can live as conflict-free as I do (or, at least, as conflict-free as possible).

I have known Mark Goulston for many years and was quite impressed with his now bestselling book, *Just Listen*, for which I was pleased to offer an endorsement. In that classic book he taught us how listening is the secret to getting through to absolutely anyone. And it really is. . . .

But when you're dealing with "challenging" personalities and it seems like there's no way to get through to them, how do you disarm or neutralize them, let alone get them to cooperate with you? For that, Mark reached deeply into his experience as a psychiatrist and psychotherapist working with many difficult patients. Mark was so well known for working with extremely difficult patients that other psychiatrists would refer their own such patients to *him*! Add to that his experience as an FBI and police hostage-negotiation trainer, and you've got a professional whose expertise can help anyone deal with the irrational and impossible people in their lives.

Take all of that and pour it into a book free of psychobabble, with a tone that's accessible to all, and filled with stories that we can all easily identify with—and add insights, tips, tactics, and tools that you can use immediately to deal more effectively with anyone in your life—and that's the magic that you have in your hands. Because with *Talking to "Crazy"* you'll be able to eliminate the stress that any difficult relationships are now causing you.

When you do that, you too might say, "Life is good."

Marshall Goldsmith

SECTION 1

The Basics of
Talking to "Crazy"

To reach irrational people, you need to know why they're irrational.

What's more, you need to know why arguing or reasoning with crazy doesn't work, while leaning into the crazy does.

chapter 1

Understanding Crazy

AFTER DECADES as a psychiatrist, I know crazy—and that includes some serious crazy.

How serious? One of my patients stalked Britney Spears, and another jumped off a fifth-story balcony because he thought he could fly. Still another called me from a jail in the Dominican Republic, saying he was there to start a revolution.

In addition, I've worked with 80-pound anorexics, strung-out heroin addicts, and hallucinating schizophrenics. I've taught hostage negotiators how to get homicidal criminals to surrender. And these days, I show CEOs and managers how to deal with out-of-control people who threaten their companies' bottom lines.

In short, crazy and I are pretty much on a first-name basis.

However, a while ago, something occurred to me: I expect to deal with crazy every day, because it's my job. But I suddenly realized how often *you* have to face down crazy—not the jump-off-a-balcony, stalk-Britney-Spears kind of crazy, but what I call everyday crazy.

My "aha" moment occurred when I went to a meeting for estate planners who needed advice about helping families in crisis. I expected the event to be a little dry, but instead, I was mesmerized. I found out that just like me, these people have to "talk to crazy" every day. In fact, nearly every issue they discussed involved clients acting completely nuts.

These lawyers had no trouble writing wills and creating trusts. But what they didn't know, and desperately needed to know, was what to do when they can't stop their clients from acting crazy.

That's when it dawned on me that everyone—including you—has this problem. I'm betting that nearly every day, you deal with at least one irrational person. Maybe it's a boss who wants the impossible. Maybe it's a demanding parent or a hostile teen or a manipulative coworker or a neighbor who's always in your face. Maybe it's a tearful lover or an unreasonable client.

And that's what this book is all about: talking to "crazy."

Now, a word about the word *crazy*: I know it sounds inflammatory and totally un-PC. But when I use this word, I don't mean mentally ill (although mental illness—which I'll address separately in Section 5—certainly causes crazy behavior). And I don't use the word *crazy* to stigmatize one group of people either. That's because all of us, at some points in time, are crazy.

What I mean by *crazy* is irrational. There are four ways in which the people you deal with can be irrational:

▶ They can't see the world clearly.

▶ They say or think things that make no sense.

▶ They make decisions and take actions that aren't in their best interest.

▶ They become downright impossible when you try to guide them back to the side of reason.

In this book, I'll share my best tricks for breaking through to people who are irrational in these ways. I've used these techniques to do everything from settling office feuds to rescuing marriages, and you can use them just as effectively to handle the irrational people in your life.

The Key: Leaning into the Crazy

The tools I'll give you in this book take some courage to implement. That's because you aren't going to make crazy go away by ignoring it, trying to reason with it, or arguing with it. Instead, you're going to lean into the crazy.

Years ago, someone gave me the following advice about how to react if a dog sinks its teeth into your hand: If you give in to your instincts and try to pull your hand out, the dog will stick its teeth in deeper. But if you counterintuitively push your hand deeper into the dog's mouth, the dog will release it. Why? Because, in order to do what it wants to do next—swallow—it has to release its jaw. And that's when you can pull your hand out.

This exact same rule applies to talking to irrational people. If you treat them as if they're nuts and you're not, they'll bite down deeper on their crazy thinking. But if you lean into their crazy, you'll radically change the dynamic. Here's an example.

After a horrific day—one of the most frustrating in my life—I was wrapped up in my woes while driving home from work on autopilot. Unfortunately, that's incredibly dangerous in California rush-hour traffic.

Just as I was entering the San Fernando Valley going south on Sepulveda Boulevard, I accidentally cut off a large man and his wife in a pickup truck. He honked angrily at me, and I waved to gesture I was sorry. Then, a half a mile later—idiotically—I proceeded to do it again.

At that point, the man caught up to me and pulled his truck to an abrupt stop in front of me, forcing me off the road. As I stopped, I could see the man's wife gesturing frantically to him not to get out of the truck.

But he didn't listen to her, and in a few moments, he did get out—all six and a half feet and 300 pounds of him. He stormed over to my car and banged wildly on my side window, screaming obscenities at me.

I was so dazed that I actually rolled my window down to hear him. Then I just waited until he paused to reload on more vitriol.

And at that moment, as he stopped to take a breath, I said to him:

"Have you ever had such an awful day that you're just hoping to meet someone who will pull out a gun, shoot you, and put you out of your misery? Are you that someone?"

His mouth fell open. "What?" he asked.

Up to that point, I'd been incredibly stupid. But in that instant, I did something brilliant. Somehow, in the midst of my brain fog, I said exactly the right thing.

I didn't try to reason with this terrifying man, who probably would have responded by dragging me out of my car and smashing his fist into my face. And I didn't fight back. Instead, I leaned into his crazy and threw it right back at him.

As the man stared at me, I started up again. "Yeah, I really mean it. I don't usually cut people off, and I never cut someone off twice. I'm just having a day where no matter what I do or who I meet— including you!—I seem to mess everything up. Are you the person who is going to mercifully put an end to it?"

Instantly, a change came over him. He switched to being calming and reassuring: "Hey. C'mon, man," he said. "It'll be okay. Really! Just relax, it'll be okay. Everyone has days like this."

I continued my rant. "That's easy for you to say! You didn't screw up everything like I did today. I don't think it will be okay. I just want out! Can't you help me with that?"

He continued with fervor: "No, really. I mean it. It'll be okay. Just relax."

We talked for a few more minutes. Then he got back into his truck, said a few things to his wife, and waved to me in the rearview mirror as if to say, "Now remember. Relax. It'll be okay."

And he drove off.

Now, I'm not proud of this episode. Clearly, the guy in the pickup truck wasn't the only irrational person on the road that day.

But here's my point. That guy could have punched my lights out. And he probably would have if I'd tried to use reason or to argue with him. Instead, I met him in his reality, in which I was the bad guy and he had every right to hurt me. By instinctively using a technique I call *assertive submission* (which I'll talk about in Chapter 8), I turned him from an assailant into an ally in less than a minute.

Luckily, my response came naturally, even on that really bad day. That's because I've been leaning into people's crazy for years as a psychiatrist. I've done it thousands of times, in different ways, and I know that it works.

Moreover, I know that it can work for you. Leaning into crazy is a strategy you can use with any irrational person. For instance, you can use this strategy to talk with:

- A partner who screams at you—or refuses to speak to you

- A child who says, "I hate you" or "I hate myself"

- An aging parent who says, "You don't care about me"

- An employee who constantly melts down on the job

- A manager who's a bully

No matter what kind of everyday crazy you're dealing with, leaning into that crazy can empower you to break free from communication strategies that fail every time and break through to the people you need to reach. As a result, you'll be able to walk into just about any emotional situation—anywhere—and feel confident, in control, and unafraid.

Replacing Fight-or-Flight with the Sanity Cycle

One thing to understand is that leaning into the crazy doesn't come instinctively. That's because it's what your body doesn't want you to do.

When you're dealing with an irrational person, your body sends you danger signals. Pay attention, and you'll notice that your throat tightens, your pulse speeds up, you get a sick feeling in your stomach, or you develop a headache. In fact, just the mention of the person's name may make you react physiologically.

This is your reptile brain (which I'll discuss further in Chapter 2) telling you either to fight, flee, or freeze. But if the irrational person is part of your professional or personal life, none of these responses will solve your problem.

Instead, I'm going to teach you how to approach crazy very differently, using a six-step process I call the Sanity Cycle (see Figure 1–1).

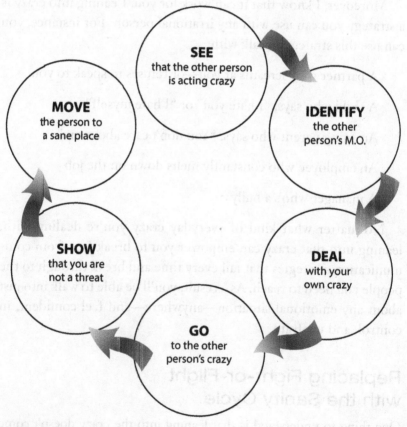

SEE
that the other person
is acting crazy

MOVE
the person to
a sane place

IDENTIFY
the other
person's M.O.

SHOW
that you are
not a threat

DEAL
with your
own crazy

GO
to the other
person's crazy

FIGURE 1-1: The Sanity Cycle

Here's what you'll do at each step of this cycle:

1. Recognize that the person you're dealing with isn't able to think rationally in the current situation. In addition, you'll realize that the person's crazy has deep roots in either the recent or distant past rather than the present moment, and that it isn't something you can argue or reason away.

2. Identify the person's modus operandi—the specific way he acts out his crazy. This is the strategy he uses to make you crazy, by causing you to become angry, guilty, ashamed, afraid, frustrated, or otherwise crazy yourself. When you understand the person's M.O., you'll feel calmer, more centered, and more in control when the two of you interact—and you'll be able to select the right counterstrategy.

3. Realize that the crazy behavior isn't about you. Instead, it's all about the person you're dealing with. To keep yourself from taking his words personally, you'll identify and neutralize many of your buttons before talking with him. And while talking with the person, you'll use powerful mental tools to keep yourself from escalating into crazy. These tools will allow you to prevent an *amygdala hijack* (a term coined by psychologist Daniel Goleman), which occurs when your amygdala—the threat-sensing part of your brain—blocks out your rational mind.

4. Talk with the irrational person, leaning into his crazy by entering his world calmly and with intention. First, you will assume innocence. That is, you'll believe that the person is truly good at heart and that there's a reason for the crazy behavior. Rather than being judgmental, you will be curious about what underlies that behavior. Second, you'll imagine yourself experiencing those underlying emotions—feeling attacked, misunderstood, and defensive.

5. Show the person that you are an ally rather than a threat by listening calmly and empathetically as he vents. Rather than shutting him down, you'll encourage this venting. And rather than attacking back, as the person expects, you'll align yourself with him. In fact, you'll even apologize to him. As you listen kindly and mirror the person empathetically, he'll begin to listen to and mirror you.

6. Help guide the person to a saner way of thinking when he is calm.

The majority of the techniques I'll teach you in this book follow these steps (although there are variations, and you'll sometimes veer completely off this path when you're dealing with bullies, manipulators, or sociopaths). That's because the Sanity Cycle is powerful magic.

Be aware, however, that guiding yourself and an irrational person through this cycle won't always be easy, won't always be fun, and won't always work instantly. And, as with anything you do in life, there's a risk that it won't work—even a very slight chance that you will make things worse. But when you desperately need to find a way to get through to a person who's difficult, impossible, or even completely out of control, these techniques will give you your very best shot.

So if you're game, I'm game. However, before we get to my techniques for talking to "crazy," I'd like to talk a little about why people act irrationally. First, we'll look at what's happening in their minds right now—and what's happened to them in the past.

chapter 2

Recognizing How Crazy Happens

TO SUCCESSFULLY talk to crazy, you need to know why irrational people act the way they do. And the first step in understanding these people is to recognize that they're a lot more like flat-out insane people than you think.

Take a moment to think about psychotic people, such as those with untreated schizophrenia or delusional depression. You know you can't reason these people's problems away. You're not going to say, "You know you're not really the Antichrist, right?" or "Your life isn't that bad, so take the gun out of your mouth and go mow the lawn."

However, I'm guessing that this is exactly the approach you take with the everyday crazies in your life. That's because you think that somehow you can simply reason their crazy away. For instance, you may say things such as:

- "Calm down—you're overreacting."

- "That doesn't make any sense."

- "You can't seriously believe that. Here are the facts."

- "Get real . . . that's just nuts!"

- "Wait a minute . . . how did you come up with *that*?"

I'm sure you've heard the popular definition of insanity: doing the same thing over and over and expecting a different result. Well, if you're trying to reason with irrational people in this way, over and over, despite not getting the response you want, guess what: You're the one who's crazy.

Why? Because garden-variety craziness, just like real psychosis, isn't just something you can talk people out of. It doesn't respond to facts or logic. And if you keep trying to reason with irrational people, they won't just suddenly snap out of it.

It's not that they refuse to change. It's that they can't. Most people who behave irrationally aren't even remotely psychotic, but like psychotic people, they're unable to think sanely. That's because crazy thoughts and behavior stem from a misalignment of the brain (or more accurately, the three brains), and a misaligned brain can't respond to reason.

The Science Behind Crazy

To understand crazy, you need to know a little about how it develops. So here's a quick look at how the mind works, and how it gets crazy.

First, you should know that what you think of as your mind actually uses three brains to function. These three brains interconnect, but they often operate on their own. Sometimes they're at war with each other. Under stress, sometimes they disconnect from each other. They always disconnect when people are truly distressed. And they often realign in ways that leave irrational people trapped in crazy.

Neuroscientist Paul McLean, who first described the triune, or three-part, brain back in the 1960s, outlined his model in depth in his 1990 book *The Triune Brain in Evolution*. Here's a look at the three brains and what they do:

▶ First and innermost is your primitive lower brain. Also known as the reptilian brain, its focus is pure survival: food, sex, escape, or attack.

> The next part of your brain is the paleomammalian middle brain, where emotions such as joy, hate, protectiveness, sadness, and pleasure arise. It's also the part of the brain that makes you bond with a partner or child.

> The outer part of your brain is your neomammalian upper brain. The most evolved of your three brains, it allows you to make smart decisions, plan ahead, and control your impulses. Most of all, it lets you look at a situation objectively instead of subjectively.

The brains develop at different stages, and each one lies on the previous one.

At birth, all three of your brains already exist. If you're lucky, they align in a healthy way over time, allowing you to mesh your survival instincts, emotions, and logical thought processes. When this occurs, each of your three brains can take charge at the right moments, and they can work together collaboratively, with your most evolved brain running the show most of the time. I call this *triunal agility*. If you possess triunal agility, you can approach a situation in one way, but if the situation changes, you can release your three brains from their alignment, consider the new situation, realign your brains with the new reality, and then succeed by dealing with it differently.

If you achieve triunal agility, you become adaptable and resilient. As a result, you can deal with whatever life throws at you—even big upsets and tragedies. Occasionally you'll slide into crazy when an upset causes your three brains to temporarily misalign, but you won't live there permanently.

What happens, however, if your early life experiences make your brains align in a less healthy way—for example, if your three brains align to think, "It's not safe to speak freely," because you were raised by a harshly critical parent? If this happens over and over, you'll begin to believe that the world isn't safe, and you'll be fearful and inhibited around people beyond your critical parent—for instance, a classroom teacher who's asking you a question.

In this case, your three brains have become locked and aligned as if you're constantly facing your parent, are feeling criticized, and are thinking that it's not safe to give a wrong answer. As a result, you may say nothing, or say fearfully, "I don't know." Your brain has become locked in *triunal rigidity*, and your thoughts, feelings, and actions will tend to fall into the same pattern in any situation that makes you flash back to your critical parent. In the psychological world, we call this *transference*, because you're transferring the way you think about people who aren't present onto the person with whom you're interacting.

In triunal rigidity, your three brains become aligned with a reality that isn't the one you're currently facing. This leaves you trapped in thought patterns that don't make sense in the present and stops you from accurately processing changes in the future. The result? Chronically crazy behavior—that is, doing the same things over and over and expecting a new reality to change back into the old reality in which those things worked.

Three Pathways to Crazy (and One to Sane)

Because crazy starts with a misaligned brain, you need to approach it not from the outside in—by bombarding it with facts—but from the inside out. But to do that, you'll need a little background on how some of the most common forms of crazy get embedded in people's minds early in their lives.

First, many people are born prewired in ways that can contribute to crazy. For instance, if people's genes make them prone to anxiety or pessimism or emotionality, the path to crazy may be a little shorter for them.

Second, and equally important, people's early experiences shape how crazy or how sane they become. Here's how it works:

Life is a series of steps into the unknown. Every time we take a step into that unknown, we confront a challenge. This challenge can make us feel excited, anxious, or both. And it can make us experience separation anxiety when we move away from what's known and safe.

As we get more comfortable with being separate, we start to experience a different feeling: individuation anxiety. We break free of childhood, but we begin to worry about whether we can make it to the other side and succeed as adults. This is a normal part of growing up.

Throughout this journey, we look back at the people who matter to us. When we step forward and triumph, we look back for that "Good for you—you can do it!" And when we step forward and hit a wall, we look for a response that reassures us so we can get back up and take another step. In this way, we keep moving ahead: two steps forward and occasionally one step back, because normal development is a matter of trial and error. The process looks like Figure 2–1.

But what happens if we look back for support and don't get it? We become less confident about stepping into the unknown. We succeed less and fail more. We move two steps forward and three steps back.

If we fall into this pattern, we begin to lose the ability to grow and adapt. Instead, we become locked in triunal rigidity. And, to a large or small degree, we become crazy.

There are three pathways to the failure that leads to craziness, and one pathway to sanity. Here's a look at each of them.

Fail #1: *Coddling*

Do you know people who chronically whine, try to manipulate you, or expect applause every time they do the tiniest task? Odds are, this was their path to crazy.

Coddling comes in different forms. Some caregivers rush in to help whenever a child gets upset. Others constantly overpraise kids for doing something well, or make excuses for them when they act badly. These caregivers equate coddling with loving and caring. But in reality, they're setting up kids for a fall when the world doesn't treat them as special.

Those who have been coddled often develop a form of crazy in which they tell themselves, "Someone will do things for me." Consequently, they feel entitled to success and happiness without having

FIGURE 2-1: How Personality Develops

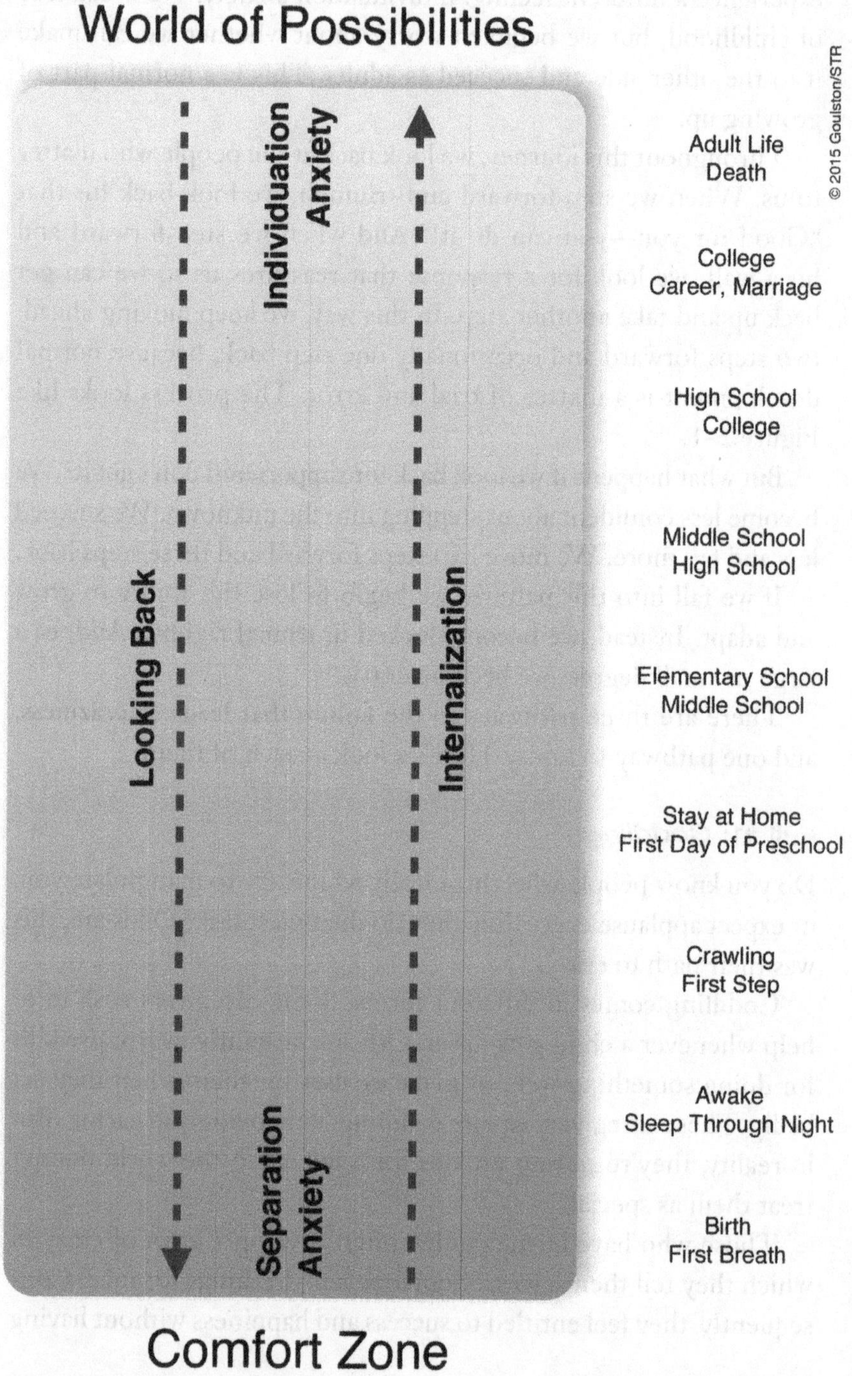

World of Possibilities

© 2015 Goulston/STR

Individuation
Anxiety

Looking Back

Internalization

Separation
Anxiety

Adult Life
Death

College
Career, Marriage

High School
College

Middle School
High School

Elementary School
Middle School

Stay at Home
First Day of Preschool

Crawling
First Step

Awake
Sleep Through Night

Birth
First Breath

Comfort Zone

to earn it. They're also prone to addictive behaviors, because they want to bail themselves out of bad moods rather than put in the effort required to find positive solutions.

Fail #2: *Criticizing*

Do you deal with any angry, bitter blamers? There's a good chance that whenever these people looked for support in their younger years, they got criticism instead. And as a result, they felt a pain that quickly crossed over into anger.

Children who endure constant criticism can grow into adolescents who take revenge by doing things that embarrass the adults in their lives. Or they may take their anger out in other ways: by bullying, driving recklessly, cutting themselves, or covering themselves in piercings.

What happens later in life when these people hit obstacles? They feel like victims, but all they know is blame and criticism, so they tend to become blamers themselves. Eventually, they become unforgiving and bitter.

Because of the constant criticism these people heard as children, their form of crazy is, "No matter what I do, I'll never be good enough." Even when they do experience success, instead of being able to savor the moment, they think that all it earns them is a pass for that day, until the whole never-good-enough cycle returns. And that makes them even angrier at the world.

Fail #3: *Ignoring*

When people react to every idea you offer with "It won't work," it's a good bet that they had caregivers who ignored them. These caregivers may have been narcissists. Or perhaps they were exhausted, ill, or overwhelmed. Maybe they were foster parents who provided care *for* these people but didn't really care *about* them.

When children look back after a triumph and find that the adults in their lives didn't even notice, or when they look back in defeat and see that their caregivers are focused on their own interests or pain instead, their response is fear. And worse yet, they realize that they're alone in their fear. This leads to a pessimistic, defeatist, it'll-never-work attitude. They grow terrified of taking a chance, falling on their faces, and reexperiencing the feeling of being alone in fear that they felt as children.

The form of crazy that these people develop is, "I'd better not take any chances or do anything that's risky."

The Ideal: *Supporting*

Think of the sanest people in your life, the people you'd describe as poised, wise, emotionally intelligent, kind, or good. In my experience, most of these people had childhoods that made them strong and resilient.

These people were lucky because when they looked back after a triumph or defeat, they received support. If it didn't come from their parents, they had the good fortune to receive it from teachers, mentors, or coaches.

These people weren't coddled, ruthlessly criticized, or ignored. Instead, their mentors taught, guided, and coached them. These adults weren't perfect—that's too high a standard to hold anyone to—but they provided what I call "good enough nurturing."

When people have mentors like this, they grow up feeling safe and confident. As a result, they develop a strong core. When they're faced with new challenges, they think, "I can do this." That's because they've internalized their loving mentors' support. When they have setbacks, they don't resort to whining, blaming someone, or withdrawing. Instead, they're determined. Their operating principle is, "Look out world—here I come."

These people will still act crazy at times, because we all do. But for them, crazy will be a temporary situation, not a way of life.

(By the way, if you didn't receive supportive parenting, the situation is far from hopeless. A good coach, teacher, or mentor can retrofit you with a healthy mindset, which is what happened to me. So if you experienced coddling, criticism, or neglect as a child, look for people who can nurture you now.)

See Figure 2–2 for another way of looking at the three paths to crazy behavior and the one path to sanity.

FIGURE 2–2: What Personality Becomes

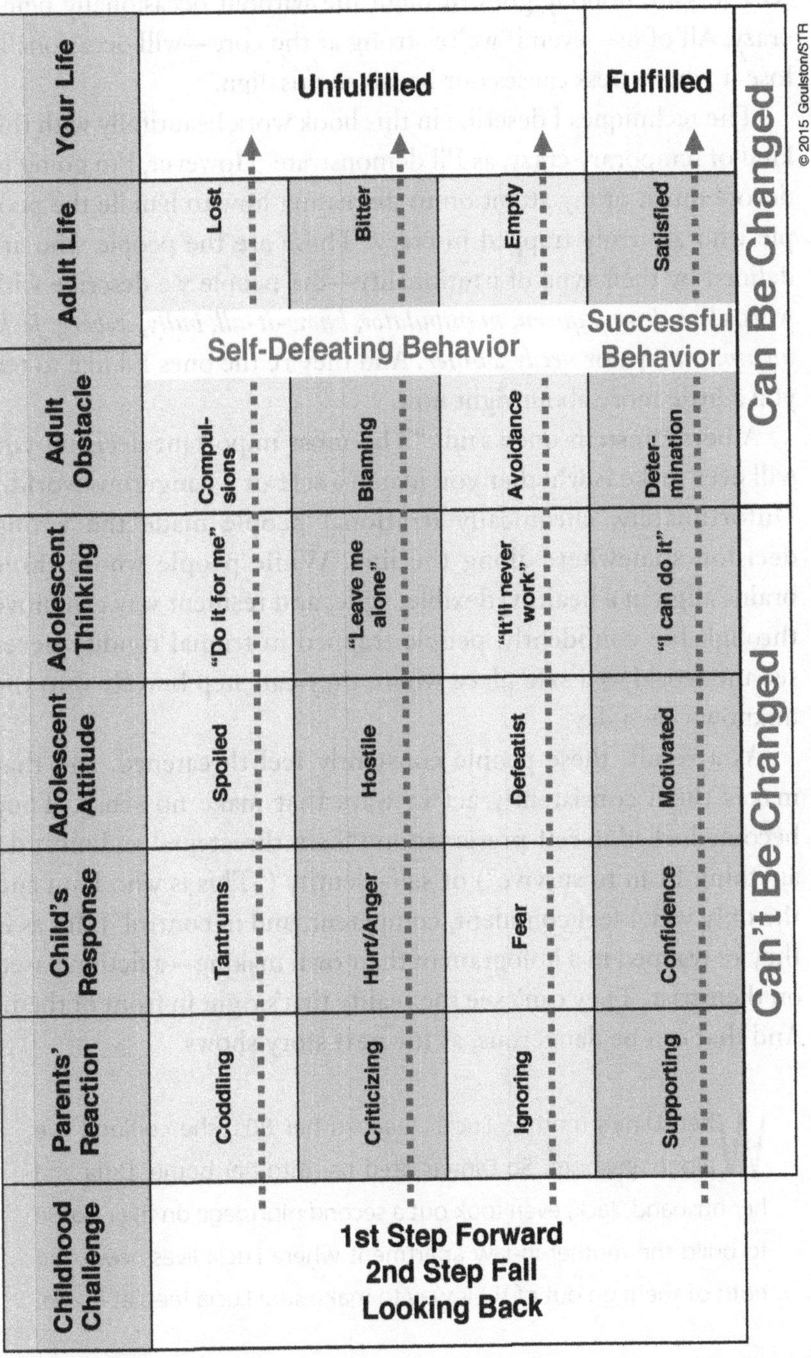

© 2015 Goulston/STR

Your Life	**Unfulfilled**			**Fulfilled**
Adult Life	Lost	Bitter	Empty	Satisfied
	Self-Defeating Behavior			**Successful Behavior**
Adult Obstacle	Compulsions	Blaming	Avoidance	Determination
Adolescent Thinking	"Do it for me"	"Leave me alone"	"It'll never work"	"I can do it"
Adolescent Attitude	Spoiled	Hostile	Defeatist	Motivated
Child's Response	Tantrums	Hurt/Anger	Fear	Confidence
Parents' Reaction	Coddling	Criticizing	Ignoring	Supporting
Childhood Challenge	1st Step Forward / 2nd Step Fall / Looking Back			

Can Be Changed

Can't Be Changed

Temporary Versus Chronic Crazy

As I've said, nobody goes through life without occasionally being crazy. All of us—even if we're strong at the core—will occasionally lose it when stress causes our brains to misalign.

The techniques I describe in this book work beautifully with this kind of temporary crazy, as I'll demonstrate. However, I'm going to devote much of my attention to discussing how to handle the people who are truly trapped in crazy. These are the people who are defined by their type of irrationality—the people we describe with words like *drama queen, manipulator, know-it-all, bully, iceberg, jerk, victim, martyr*, or *needy whiner*. And they're the ones I'd like to tell you a little more about right now.

Albert Einstein once said, "The most important decision you will ever make is whether you live in a safe or a dangerous world." Unfortunately, chronically irrational people made the wrong decision somewhere along the line. While people whose three brains align in a healthy, flexible, agile, and resilient way can move through life confidently, people trapped in triunal rigidity never see the world as a safe place where they can step bravely into the unknown each day.

As a result, these people constantly feel threatened, and that makes them consistently act in ways that make no sense. They become locked in self-preservation ("I am threatened and must do anything I can to survive") or self-identity ("This is who I am and the only way I feel confident, competent, and in control"). It's as if they're trapped in a hologram of their own making—a fiction based on their past. They can't see the reality that's right in front of them. And that can be dangerous, as my next story shows.

When Dina's mother, Lucia, reached her 80s, she couldn't live alone anymore. So Dina invited her into her home. Dina and her husband, Jack, even took out a second mortgage on their house to build the mother-in-law apartment where Lucia lives now. And both of them go out of their way to make sure Lucia feels at home.

So how's it working out?

According to Dina, "It's hell."

The first words out of Lucia's mouth every day and her last words at night are, "You're a terrible daughter or you wouldn't make me live with that man. You don't care about me. You want me to die."

One night, she told Jack, "You want to get rid of me. But you won't win. You're going to die first."

Clearly, Lucia is irrational. She's lucky to have a family who's willing to take her in and keep her safe. And she's going to end up in a nursing home if she keeps hurting Dina and alienating Jack. Everything she's doing is crazy.

Why does Lucia act the way she does? Because her three brains are misaligned, and she can't think rationally.

Lucia grew up in a poor and abusive family from which she escaped by marrying young. When she and her husband decided to come to America, an uncle took them in. But eight weeks later, the uncle changed his mind and threw them out. They were stuck in a strange country where they didn't speak the language—and Lucia was five months pregnant.

Lucia's husband got a job as a dishwasher and worked his way up to restaurant manager. But he also became an alcoholic and eventually drank himself to death, leaving her alone to raise three kids.

As a result of her early experiences, Lucia never developed a strong core. Instead, she's wired to be fearful and suspicious. She lives in constant terror, with her reptile brain dominating and blocking the input from her logical and emotional brains. Seeing the world as a dangerous place, and always expecting other people to leave or betray her, she is fixed on self-preservation.

In Lucia's mind, Dina is the key to her survival. And the other people Dina cares about—Jack, for instance—aren't good people but rather threats to that survival. From her perspective, Jack is stealing Dina's attention and loyalty. And worse yet, she's afraid Jack might convince Dina to abandon her. (Ironically, he might, if Lucia keeps behaving this badly.)

So Lucia lashes out at Dina and Jack out of irrational fear. And no amount of reasoning will ever get through to her, because her three brains simply can't comprehend the reality that's right in front of her.

Lucia is in a bad place right now, and things are likely to get worse. That's because the longer people stay trapped in old and no-longer-relevant thought patterns, the more they resist facts and logic.

It's as if a chronically irrational person's mind is a compass aimed permanently at magnetic north. If life calls for these people to move even slightly east, west, or south, they dig their heels in, convinced that only north exists—and that if they move an inch, they will lose all control over their lives or even die.

What we see as resistance to change, these people see as persistence. They persist in knowing what they know and believing what they believe, no matter how unhelpful or unrelated to reality. In effect, they're diligently guarding the only territory they have. The more these people's brains misalign with their current reality, the more fiercely they will defend this territory, and the crazier they will get. That's because the greater the misalignment, the more out of touch they will become without anything in the real world to anchor them. As a result, the anxiety they feel can rapidly escalate to panic. And when that happens they can become desperate.

Clearly, when these people feel panicky and become desperate, they are operating in a very different reality than yours, and this means you can't talk with them the way you would with a rational person. That's because while two plus two equals four in your world, it may just as clearly and unarguably equal six in theirs. This is true for temporary crazy as well, but it's even truer for those who are chronically irrational.

And this is why you'll never be able to reason chronically irrational people out of their crazy. Instead, as I mentioned in Chapter 1, you'll need to lean into that crazy. That is, you're going to enter the land in which two plus two equals six, and you're going to state your case there.

But to do that, there's one more thing you need to know: What kind of crazy is the person you're dealing with? To answer that question, you'll need to identify the person's modus operandi, or M.O.

chapter 3

Spotting an Irrational Person's M.O.

EVERY MURDERER has a modus operandi—a preferred way of operating. One killer uses a knife, another uses a bomb, and a third goes for a bullet to the back of the head.

Similarly, all irrational people sport their own brand of crazy. This is how they get you to do what they want, while resisting doing what you want.

In Chapter 2, I told you about Lucia, who's holding her family hostage with her bullying. Lucia's M.O. is to attack people wildly. Other irrational people may cry, withdraw, become ice-cold, act sarcastic, or whine.

Why do these people behave the way they do? To stay in control. As I mentioned in Chapter 2, irrational people—especially those who are firmly in the grip of crazy—are terrified of losing control. To avoid this, they subconsciously try to get *you* to lose control by creating an amygdala hijack in you. As discussed in Chapter 1, this occurs when your amygdala, a threat-sensing region in your middle, emotional brain, hijacks you away from using your prefrontal cortex—the region at the front of your frontal lobes, where logic and reason hold sway—and instead throws you into your lower, reptilian, fight-or-flight brain.

If these people succeed, you'll become very emotional and have trouble thinking straight. Eventually, you'll either melt down or escape. And that means you'll lose any chance of getting the person to come around to your way of thinking.

An irrational person's M.O. is a weapon. However, it's also a weakness because if you can figure out the person's M.O., you can turn this information to your advantage. An M.O. makes the person predictable, so you'll know what to expect—whether it's tears, screaming, silence, or bullying. And when you're prepared, it'll be easier for you to keep your own amygdala reined in.

From Identity to M.O.

Irrational people's M.O.s are outward projections of their inner identities—the way they see themselves and their relationship to the world as a result of their early experiences. For example:

- People who were coddled often are needy or manipulative or become highly emotional when they're expected to do something they don't want to do.

- People who were constantly criticized often become bullies or know-it-alls, or become rigidly logical and practical.

- People who were ignored tend to be fearful, withdrawn, or hopeless—or become martyrs, because they're accustomed to not receiving help when they ask for it.

Even people who were supported during childhood can become emotional, withdrawn, cold, or fearful when they feel they're under attack; but in general, they don't like confrontations any more than you do, so they're likely to back down before they push you into a full-fledged amygdala hijack.

The crazier people are, the more rigid their M.O.s will be. As a result, identifying an irrational person's M.O. is often more simple than you'd think. Figure 3–1 shows the M.O.s you're most likely to encounter when you talk to crazy.

FIGURE 3–1: The Nine Most Common M.O.s of Irrational People

M.O.s of Irrational People

Irrational Person's M.O.		Your Reaction
Emotional	Emotional people believe they need to vent or they'll explode. Therefore they cry, scream, and slam doors. They tend to overpower you because they're willing to escalate a situation to a point that's unbearable for a sane person.	You may try to mollify these people by giving in to them so you can stop the unending emotional upheaval, or you may become so tired of it all that you just try to escape from them.
Logical/Practical	These people think they're in control only when they stick to the facts. As a result, they become terse, cold, and condescending. They tune out anything that seems illogical and nearly always view displays of emotion as "acting crazy."	You may start feeling and acting more emotional and angry in response to these people's dry and logical statements and the way they cut you off with icy logic. They also have a way of causing you to feel ashamed of even having feelings.
Manipulative/ Needy	These people believe that to be in control, they need something from you that they can't supply themselves. So they whine, wheedle, and make excuses. If you suggest ways they can help themselves, they say, "Yes, but . . ." If you don't give them what they want, often they try to control you by making you feel guilty.	When these people are unrelenting, you may transition from feeling guilty and frustrated to feeling annoyed, put-upon, and ashamed of your deep desire to say something mean to them. You may give in to them just to get rid of them—even though you know they'll just come back for more.

Irrational Person's M.O.		Your Reaction
Fearful	Fearful people feel like they're constantly surrounded by threats. When something triggers their fear, they lash out wildly like a frightened dog. They also are much more comfortable than you being perched between fear and panic (because they are there so often).	These people evoke in you a nearly constant need to reassure them, which eventually gets exhausting and makes you resent them. If you go the extra mile to walk them through fearful situations, you're likely to find yourself becoming a regular crutch because they can't or won't move a step without you.
Hopeless/ Withdrawn	Hopeless/withdrawn people feel that the world will only hurt them, so their M.O. is to hide from it. No matter how hard you try to convince these people that they can be happy in the future, they spend enormous amounts of energy trying to convince you that you're wrong and that nothing will work.	These people's negativity may leave you feeling frustrated, sad, and a bit hopeless yourself. Trying to help them increases your chances of becoming part of their downer cycle as they suck the energy out of you.
Martyred	People who play the role of martyrs make a point of refusing to ask for help, even when they desperately need it.	These people initially make you feel guilty for not helping, even though they won't give you a chance. Over time, however, their martyr act can make you feel annoyed and exasperated.

(continued)

Irrational Person's M.O.		Your Reaction
Bullying	Bullies believe they're in control only if they're making you fearful and submissive. That's why they actively attack, threaten, or belittle you. The more afraid they make you feel, the more powerful they feel.	These people make you feel scared, intimidated, weak, and powerless— as well as angry. You may strike back, steam inside, or simply retreat and ruminate about what you could have done instead.
Know-It-All	Know-it-alls like being the only expert on any topic, even if they've never "been there" or "done that." They will find cracks in any idea you offer, even if it's correct. They know that if they can make you feel stupid, you'll lose confidence and often back off and become submissive. Their M.O. is to belittle, mock, or condescend to you.	These people may make you feel small, insignificant, not good enough, and sometimes ashamed—as well as resentful.
Sociopathic	These people (who technically are sane, but often are irrational in a unique way you'll read about later) are hiding secrets. Their M.O. is to terrify you so you won't find out what those secrets are (or worse yet, expose them to the rest of the world).	These people will make you feel afraid and even "creeped out."

When you understand irrational people's M.O.s, it'll be easier for you to realize that their weeping, coldness, whining, withdrawal, or attack-dog behavior isn't really about you. Instead, it's about them and their need to feel in control. Moreover, as you'll see, knowing a person's M.O. will show you the best way to counter it.

Stephen had a subordinate named Harry who drove him crazy. No matter what Stephen suggested, Harry always found a way to say, "Yes, but . . ." Every day, Harry had a reason why he couldn't get things done.

When I asked Stephen why he put up with Harry, he smiled and said, "His last name is on the top of the building." Harry, Stephen explained, was the son of the company's owner.

Stephen said that no matter what advice he offered Harry, it had no effect. I explained that this behavior is classic for needy people, who will veto almost any suggestion that might make things better for them.

Harry's previous managers had a history of letting him under-perform and make excuses because nobody wanted to criticize the boss's son. But Stephen had some big targets he wanted to reach, and he needed everyone in his department to step up. "And Harry really is good at what he does," Stephen told me, "when he does it."

I told Stephen that simply criticizing Harry—his previous approach—wouldn't work. Instead, I said, the best way to deal with needy people like this is to lean into their crazy by realizing that from their point of view, it makes perfect sense. From Harry's perspective, he got other people to solve his problems while still earning a good salary and keeping his father's approval. The only way to nudge his behavior in the right direction was to come up with a consequence worse than doing his work. To accomplish this, however, Stephen had to select the right consequence.

In Harry's case, firing wasn't an option. So we talked about other ideas. One thing Stephen mentioned was that while Harry didn't care about earning his team members' respect, he did care a great deal about his father's opinion of him and about disappointing or, worse yet, angering him. Unfortunately, Harry's previous managers had glossed over Harry's failings with his CEO dad, who had no idea how poor Harry's work actually was. No wonder Harry felt safe underperforming.

I asked Stephen, "What's your plan?"

Stephen thought about it. "I can explain to Harry," he said, in a friendly and empathetic tone of voice, "that to help him ramp up his performance, I'm going to use a new approach. Going forward, I'm going to anticipate that he'll do the work I give him, because I know he's smart and capable. If he doesn't do what I ask, I'll assign someone else to do it. And once that other person does the task, I'll rewrite the roles and responsibilities to reflect it.

"I'll explain to Harry that each time he drops the ball, I'll do the same thing. And I'll carefully document all of this. And I'll tell him that if I eventually give all of his responsibilities to other people, I'll talk with his father about it. I'll show his father all of my documentation, so he can see that my team and I tried our best to work with Harry. And his dad and I will talk together about whether there's a job in the company that might suit Harry better."

Stephen was a little skeptical about how successful his plan would be. But he figured that even if Harry didn't shape up, his careful documentation would protect his own job. "And if nothing else," he said, "I'll probably get rid of Harry."

But guess what: When Harry couldn't slack off without worrying about having to face Daddy's disappointment, he began to perform. And while he never became a superstar, at least he pulled his own weight.

As you can see, identifying an irrational person's M.O. gives you considerable power over him. It also allows you to lean into his crazy confidently rather than timidly. That's why whenever possible you want to do this *before* talking to "crazy."

Take some time right now to examine the behavior of the irrational people in your life. What do these people do each time they feel threatened? Do they cry? Lash out? Try to undercut you? Become cold and condescending?

Also, think about how these people's behavior makes you feel. Do you feel guilty? Defensive? Angry? Scared? Humiliated? Frustrated?

Often, a person's M.O. is clear. If not, here's an exercise that will help you identify it. Write out these questions (or photocopy this exercise) and your answers.

M.O. Detector

Note: There is no "official" score in this exercise. Instead, answer each question and see what your gut tells you.

1. List three situations in which the person acted in a manner that seemed irrational to you.

a. _____

b. _____

c. _____

2. Describe the person's behavior in each situation.

a. _____

b. _____

c. _____

3. Describe how you felt during each of these encounters with the person.

I felt _____

I felt _____

I felt _____

4. Describe how you felt after each of these encounters with the person.

I felt _____

I felt _____

I felt _____

5. What did you do in each of these situations?

I did this _____

I did this _____

I did this _____

6. *What were your results?*

This happened _____

This happened _____

This happened _____

7. *What do you think the person would have done in each situation if you'd refused to go along with her irrationality?*

The person would have _____

The person would have _____

The person would have _____

8. *What would have been the end result for you?*

The end result would have been _____

The end result would have been _____

The end result would have been _____

When you finish this exercise, you should have a good grasp on the person's M.O. As a result, when you get to Sections 4 and 5 (where I describe approaches to use in dealing with each of the nine different M.O.s), you'll know how to pick the right techniques to use in your situation.

In addition, you'll have a clearer understanding of how you react to the irrational person's M.O. This means that you're more likely to stay calm when the two of you interact, and you're far more likely to walk away unscathed or even score a total win.

However, there's still one big question you need to ask yourself before you decide to lean into a person's crazy:

Should you?

chapter 4

Knowing When to Talk to "Crazy" and When to Walk Away

THIS BOOK is all about dealing with people who are irrational. But if you're planning to have a conversation with someone like this, there's a question you need to ask yourself first:

Why?

Do you have a good reason for trying to engage with this person? Or would you be better off steering clear?

Often, the "why" is obvious. Maybe you love the person. Or you're so entangled financially or relationally that you can't escape.

But maybe the "why" isn't so obvious. Maybe the relationship isn't important or salvageable, and you're wasting your time trying to get through. Doing that makes your own behavior crazy.

Psychiatrists spend a lot of time trying to help people who've been hurt, humiliated, manipulated, stabbed in the back, financially ruined, or even driven nearly to the point of suicide by the irrational people in their lives. And what we know is that all too often, these diligent daughters, loyal sons, martyred spouses, and devoted friends or colleagues aren't doing themselves or the people who are driving them crazy any good. They're just throwing their own lives away.

So before you tackle the bruising challenge of talking to "crazy," make sure you have a good reason to go there. Sometimes you may decide it's better to stop trying to get through to the irrational person than to drive yourself nuts trying to get that person to accept reality. Here's an example.

Chris worked with his father in the family business. Under his direction, the business grew from an antiquated, 10-person operation to a modern, multistate corporation. But his father always said things like, "You have it easy. I built this from the ground up, and you're just getting a free ride because of my hard work."

For years, Chris put up with his father's negativity, even when the company's competitors said, "We'd love to have you join us." He also tried to avoid feeling bitter when his father compared him unfavorably to his brother, Tim, who'd flown the nest and started his own highly successful firm. Feeling that blood was thicker than water, Chris told himself that family loyalty was all-important.

One day, however, his father went too far. In addition to calling Chris a freeloader, he threw Tim's success in Chris's face. "I wish I could wave a magic wand and replace you with Tim," he said.

Chris stared at his father. Then he went to his desk, packed up all of his belongings, and went home. When he got there, he picked up the phone, called the company's biggest competitor, and said, "Do you want me?"

Out on his own, Chris succeeded brilliantly. In fact, released from his father's constant criticism, he became far more confident and developed a reputation as a bold and savvy decision maker. As a result, he wound up being promoted to vice president at his new firm.

The story could have ended happily there for Chris. However, it took an interesting turn a decade later when his mother called him. "Your father is sick," she said, "and he really needs you to help with the business. He's just too proud to tell you that."

Chris realized that his father had gone from arrogant to vulnerable. In this situation, loyalty did matter. So he said yes—but on one condition. He told his father, "Before I decide whether I'm coming back, I have a favor to ask."

His father replied, "What is it?"

Chris said, "I need you to look me in the eye and say the following: 'I'm too proud to ever say to anyone that I need them. But I need you.'"

His father, accustomed to being the one who made ultimatums, balked at first. But Chris encouraged him by saying, "It'll be okay, Dad. Just say it. I need you to say it, so I can say something to you that I've never been able to tell you."

His father finally looked Chris in the eye and said, "I've been too proud to ever say to anyone that I need them, but I need *you*." The authenticity of it caught them both by surprise, and his father's eyes spontaneously teared up.

And Chris replied, with tears in his own eyes, "That's all I ever wanted to hear from you, because you've been my hero for my entire life—but I just couldn't stop resenting you for making me feel that I didn't matter."

Chris went back to his father's company on his own terms. And one of those terms was that his father had to treat him with the respect he'd earned.

Like many people, Chris spent most of his life being the "good one" in his relationship with his father. He had a lifelong habit of accepting unacceptable behavior, and letting his family—and particularly his father—walk all over him. And in constantly trying to please his father, he undercut himself.

Does any of this ring a bell with you? If so, it's time for a serious talk—not with the irrational people in your life, but with yourself.

To start, take stock of what you should be able to expect from each irrational person in your life and what you're actually getting. Ask yourself:

▸ Can you rely on this person for emotional or psychological support, or is the person distant or even abusive?

▶ Can you rely on this person for practical help, or does the person let you down whenever you need assistance?

▶ Does the person accept responsibility for his actions or blame others?

▶ Is the person reliable or unreliable?

▶ Is the person self-reliant or needy?

In addition, ask yourself what this person should expect from you and what you're actually giving. Decide if you're doing your fair share in the relationship. Also, ask yourself if you're doing far more than your fair share, and if it's frustrating or exhausting you. When you're done with this exercise, review what you've written. Then ask yourself, based on your answers: Is this a relationship worth saving? Or should you cut this person out of your life?

Before you answer this question, however, think about your entire track record with the person. For instance, if you're dealing with a demanding parent, ask yourself:

▶ "For most of our relationship, did she do her best to support me when I needed help—or did she constantly ignore, abuse, or undermine me?"

▶ "Is this a good, loving person who's behaving this way because she is old, sick, or demented—or has this person always been nasty and negative?"

Sometimes you'll owe the person loyalty "just because." Because you're grateful for everything she did for you earlier. Because it's not her fault that a trauma or illness is making her behave irrationally. Because you love her, no matter what.

But other times, you'll discover that you're sticking with an irrational person simply because you don't want to feel like a bad person yourself. You're terrified to let yourself think, "I hate you. I want you to go away," or even, "Please die, because you're killing me." If that's the case, realize that thinking these thoughts doesn't make you a bad person. It only makes you human. And if you're feeling this way, it's a very strong sign that you need to disconnect from the person.

If you determine this is the case, forget about talking to "crazy." Instead, if you can, just walk away.

Sometimes when you walk away, the person will try to pull you back in. If this happens, you can use what I call the DNR method for escaping a relationship:

> ▶ **Do Not React**. Don't make this person's problem and responsibility your fault or responsibility. Instead, tell yourself, "This is the other person's view, the other person's problem, and the other person's responsibility."

> ▶ **Do Not Respond**. Do not say anything that the person could twist to make it your fault, problem, or responsibility. (But you can acknowledge what the person says or even say, "I'm sorry you feel that way" or "It sounds like you feel upset.")

> ▶ **Do Not Resuscitate**. Do not engage with the person in any way that will cause him to rev up and try to rehook you.

Once you implement a DNR, do not go back. At first, the person may try very hard to entrap you in a relationship again. But if you don't weaken, eventually he will most likely look for a new victim. (If not, check out my strategies in Section 3 in Chapters 10, 14, 19, and 20 for handling manipulators.)

Remember: You can't always change the people around you. But you can change the people you're around.

A Warning About Personality Disorders

In Section 5, I will tell you about what to do when irrationality is actually a mental illness. But right now, I do want to take a look at one particular group of mental illnesses: personality disorders.

If you aren't a shrink, it can be very hard to tell "normal" irrationality from a personality disorder. As a result, you may mistake personality-disordered people for run-of-the-mill irrational people and attempt to use the techniques I outline without getting assistance from a therapist.

My advice? Don't do that.

Even for professionals, people with personality disorders are extremely hard to get through to. And if you're a good-hearted amateur, these people will crush you. So don't try "talking to personality disorders" without a therapist as backup. You may think you're making progress with these people, but by the next upset, all of your work will be washed away like a footprint in the sand.

How can you tell if the person you're dealing with has a personality disorder? In general, people with personality disorders exhibit many of these characteristics:

▶ They take most comments too personally.

▶ They have unrealistic expectations of life and of you.

▶ They blame other people rather than taking responsibility for their own problems.

▶ They seldom learn from their mistakes.

▶ They rarely listen to reason.

▶ They seldom see things from others' points of view, including yours.

▶ They nearly always see themselves as right and others as wrong.

▶ They see themselves as victims.

▶ They're withdrawn, cold, suspicious, or highly emotional.

The main reason these people are so exasperating is that they take little or no responsibility for the things that go wrong in their lives while taking full credit for the good things. As a result, they see no reason to change. (Instead, they expect everyone else to change.)

The FUDCRUD Test

Here's one way to smoke out a person with a personality disorder when you're on a date or you're conducting a job interview. Ask the person what has *frustrated, upset,* or *disappointed* him in the past. (That's the FUD part.) Then, when he answers, see where he hangs the blame for his problems. For instance, does he say, "I wish I'd pursued my interest in art"? Or does he say, "I wanted to be a painter, but my family didn't support me and neither did my first wife"? If the person has a personality disorder, you'll quickly see a pattern of blaming other people . . . and that's the CRUD part that tells you this isn't a person you want to get to know better.

While people with personality disorders share the traits I've described, they behave in a variety of ways. Here's a closer look at six of the most common personality disorders.

▶ **Histrionic**. These people constantly need attention and are unhappy when anyone else takes center stage. Basically, they think of you as the audience for their drama. They're flamboyant and highly emotional, they continually need to be reassured that they're attractive, and they frequently act provocatively and seductively (and not just with you). Often, they will embarrass you in public.

▶ **Narcissistic**. These people believe it's all about them. Try to talk about your interests or needs and they'll get annoyed or possibly even become infuriated. They expect special favors and don't care if they continually inconvenience you. While some people are insensitive to others because they're oblivious, narcissists almost appear to delight in their insensitivity.

▶ **Dependent**. Garden-variety irrational people are often needy, but I'm talking here about people who are always dependent. They need constant reassurance, can't make decisions, can't function on their own, and are terrified of abandonment. Even if you enjoy feeling needed by them at first, you'll eventually begin to feel used and come to resent them.

▸ **Paranoid.** These people constantly need to know where you're going, how long you're going to be gone, and which people you're going to see. And even when you offer them reassurance, they still don't trust you. We all have moments when we overanalyze other people's motives, but if such a pattern is pervasive, it's beyond normal crazy.

▸ **Borderline.** These people live in constant crisis mode. They're always terrified that you're going to abandon them or try to control them, and they will switch in a heartbeat from idolizing you to despising you. Often, they abuse drugs or alcohol or engage in promiscuous sex. They're highly unstable and very impulsive, and they may threaten suicide or cut themselves. Perhaps the best indicator that you may be dealing with someone suffering from a borderline personality is that you're increasingly afraid of upsetting the person—and when you do, he exhibits rage of monstrous proportions.

▸ **Sociopathic.** These people are often superficially charming, but they lack compassion, empathy, remorse, or a conscience. Sometimes they do exhibit *opportunistic* empathy, meaning they can be amazingly good at tuning into your vulnerabilities—but only to exploit them. They feel it's their right to do anything they please in order to get what they want. They absolutely do not care if they hurt you—and they *will* hurt you if it's to their advantage.

If any of these types sound like the irrational person you're dealing with, don't go it alone. Instead, if this is a relationship that you need or want to preserve, consult a therapist and get an expert opinion about what you're dealing with.

If your talk with a therapist leads you to suspect that you're involved with someone who has a personality disorder, there are three things you need to realize. The first is that you aren't the cause of this person's turmoil. The second is that it's not your job to fix it. And the third is that the person needs the kind of help I talk about in Section 5. Don't try to talk to this kind of crazy alone, or you're going to get burned out—and most likely hurt as well.

Instead, consider whether you should continue your connection with a person with a personality disorder. Ask yourself if there is any reason to keep putting energy into a relationship with someone who will suck you dry. Would you continue to put money into your bank if there was no return on investment? Probably not. Instead, you'd search for another bank with a fair rate of return.

The bottom line: If you're not too heavily invested in your relationship with a personality-disordered person, consider getting out. I have to deal with people like this for a living, but you don't—and unless there's a good reason, you shouldn't.

SECTION 2

Facing Your
Own Crazy First

We're all at least a little nuts—and if you don't identify
and handle your own irrationality, you'll sabotage your
efforts to get through to the people you need to reach.
That's why the first irrational person you need to talk to
is yourself—and in this section, I'll show you how.

chapter 5

Pinpointing Your Own Crazy

SO FAR, I'VE talked about other people's crazy. But that's only half the story.

Unless you're the first entirely sane person on the planet, you're carrying around your own suitcase full of crazy. And in order to successfully face down another person's crazy, you first need to deal with your own.

This isn't a comfortable thing to contemplate. In fact, right now you may be feeling a strong urge to skip this chapter and get on to *other* people's crazy (which is much more fun to think about). However, you can't get through to another person if you aren't seeing things clearly yourself. That's a lesson I learned the hard way, early in my career.

In the second year of my psychiatric residency at UCLA Hospital, I received a page from an oncology resident. "Mr. Harding is psychotic," he told me. "He's kicking and screaming, agitated, pulling out his IVs and trying to pull out the respirator hose going down his throat. We put him in restraints and gave him a shot of Haldol to calm him down, but we need you to come up and do a consult on him."

When I arrived at Mr. Harding's room, I saw an agitated man with eyes as large as saucers, fighting at his restraints, moaning, with a respirator tube in his mouth. His eyes seemed to be screaming something at me. I introduced myself and asked, "What is it?" He moaned louder. I placed a pen in his restrained right hand and put a piece of paper next to it for him to write something, but all he could do was scribble something unreadable.

At that point, I paused and calmly said, "I'm here because you were pulling at your IVs and respirator tubes, and we need to restrain your hands and feet and give you a tranquilizer to calm you down. As soon as you're able to relax, we'll remove the restraints and stop giving you a tranquilizer."

All the while, he just kept staring at me with those wide eyes and moaning. I waited a bit longer to see if I could decipher what he was trying to say, but then I thought, "The oncology doctors appear to be right: He's psychotic."

The next day I received another page from the oncology resident. "Mr. Harding is off his respirator and calm—and he told us specifically and emphatically to page you," he said in a firm voice.

When I arrived back in Mr. Harding's room, he was a different person. Sitting upright calmly in his bed, he ordered, "Sit down!"

I did. He looked deeply into my eyes and said, "What I was trying to tell you yesterday was that a piece of the respirator tubing had broken off and was stuck in my throat." I blanched and felt a knot in my stomach as I replayed the day before. He then said, "I want you to know that before I ever go through something like that again, I will kill myself. Do you understand?"

My eyes watered with the realization that I'd screwed up and my patient had suffered terrible pain and fear as a result of my mistake. "Yes, I understand and I am very sorry."

"So we understand each other," he said. "Good."

What's the point of my story? I assumed that my patient was irrational. In fact, I assumed that he was experiencing a full-fledged psychotic break. But in reality, the only crazy person in the room was me.

My interpretation of the situation was so colored by my own viewpoint (the oncology resident says the patient is psychotic; the patient looks psychotic; my training says that a tranquilizer is the right treatment) that I failed to see what was truly happening.

Viewing reality through a distorted filter, as I did in this case, can lead to very bad outcomes—not just in medicine, but in any aspect of life. It can keep you from listening to people. It can steer you to wrong solutions. And when you're talking to "crazy," it can set you up for a big fall.

Before you tackle crazy, you need to identify the ideas that distort your view of the world. In this case, I'm talking about unconscious messages you've internalized as a result of your life experiences, especially during childhood.

In Chapter 2, I discussed how our early experiences help to define how sane we are. Ideally, we'd all receive perfect nurturing, and as a result we'd be perfectly sane. But in reality, none of us comes through our early years completely unscathed, even if we have the best of caregivers.

As a result, we all carry around some negative messages that skew the way we see reality. For instance, you may have internal messages that tell you:

- "No matter what I do, I'll never be good enough."

- "I need people to take care of me."

- "I can't trust people."

- "People will hurt me."

- "I'd better not take chances."

These hidden ideas will cloud your view of the irrational person you're trying to reach. For example, if you grew up with an abusive father, you may view a mildly irrational spouse as dangerous. Or if you were coddled, you may unconsciously feel anger toward a demented elderly parent who can no longer protect you from everything and—worse yet—is now your responsibility.

That's why before you lean into someone else's crazy, you need to take a little time to explore your own. When you identify your irrational ideas and behaviors, you'll be better equipped to view someone else's irrationality clearly.

And here's another reason to investigate your own crazy: If you're dealing with an irrational person who knows you very well—a parent, a child, or a spouse, for instance—the most powerful weapon that person will use to defend his crazy is to attack *your* crazy. Just like the irrational people you're trying to reach, you have buttons as a result of the negative messages you've internalized. Irrational people will find those buttons, and they will push them as hard and ruthlessly as they can.

Don, a colleague of mine, is one of the best "professional listeners" I know. When he's with clients, he has the patience of Job, never reacting and always remaining calm, caring, and present. However, he recently told me a story that illustrates how dangerous it can be when your buttons are pushed.

Don deeply loves his wife, Amanda. But like many husbands, he also tends to tune her out at times. What bothers Amanda most is that Don always gives his clients his full and undivided attention, but when he's with her, he often seems distracted. At these times, she feels less important to him than his clients are.

One day, thoroughly exasperated by Don's lack of interest in what she was saying, Amanda slid into crazy. She blurted out, "You're an awful listener! In fact, I don't even know how you make a living doing what you do, and why anyone would hire you!"

Amanda's harsh comments pushed one of Don's biggest buttons. More than anything, he considers himself a good listener. And Amanda had caught him with his "caring" down. Worse, she'd triggered his hidden fear of not being good enough—a leftover from years of living with a hypercritical father who always told him, "You'll never amount to anything."

Don knew better than to do what he did next—but obviously Amanda had pushed a big button. So rather than leave bad enough alone, Don forgot everything he knew about communicating and replied, "If you ever had a thought worth listening to, it would die of loneliness!"

That cost him a few nights in the den.

To help prevent situations like this, you need to inoculate yourself by identifying as many of your own negative messages as you can. When you spot them, take steps to neutralize them. Here's how: Schedule some quiet time when you can think without interruption. Then begin with the following two exercises.

Exercise 1: Back to the Future

This exercise will empower you to spot many of the crazy ideas you're carrying around in your head. When you bring these ideas from your past out into the open and analyze them, they'll begin to lose much of their hold over you. In addition, you'll be able to identify your default responses to various situations and decide if your defaults are serving you well or not. Once you've finished this exercise, you'll see things more clearly—and you'll have fewer buttons for irrational people to push.

Here's how it works.

1. Think about and then write down the most important events in your life. Make your list from these possibilities or others:

> *Your first day of school*

▶ *Summer vacations*

▶ *Experiences with brothers or sisters*

▶ *Fights you got into*

▶ *Triumphs and losses*

▶ *Your first sexual experience*

▶ *Problems with the law*

▶ *Your most embarrassing/shameful incidents*

Start chronologically and describe each event in writing. Don't edit yourself. Just write down your words as they come to your mind.

2. Wait a day and then look at your list again. Select the most positive and most negative events that happened in each of the following stages:

▶ *Your early childhood*

▶ *Your later childhood*

▶ *Your preteen years*

▶ *Your adolescence*

▶ *Your adulthood (if you are old enough, break this down into early, middle, and late adulthood)*

3. For each event, answer these questions:

▶ *What happened? What were your immediate thoughts, feelings, and reactions?*

▶ *What did the people you looked to for support do or say during or after the event? What did you think and feel as a result?*

▶ *What actions did you take, and what were the consequences?*

▶ *What beliefs did you form about yourself and the people around you, and how safe or unsafe did you feel as a result of the event?*

4. Either on your own or with the help of a friend or partner, ask yourself these questions:

- ▶ *Are the beliefs you formed during these experiences limiting how you live today?*

- ▶ *If the beliefs made sense at the moment after the event, do they serve you well now?*

- ▶ *Do the beliefs you formed after negative events seem to have more of a grip on you today than the beliefs you formed after positive events?*

- ▶ *Can you spot any buttons you have as a result of these experiences?*

- ▶ *Finally, and most important, if an event similar to one you experienced in the past happens again in the future, can you think of a new response and/or different belief that would better serve you?*

Exercise 2: Back to the Future—One More Time

For this exercise, follow the same process you did in the first exercise. However, think specifically about events that involved the irrational person you're trying to reach. As you identify your negative ideas from your past, consider how this person might use your resulting buttons against you.

One final suggestion about these two exercises: You may want to share them with your intimate partner and encourage this person to do them as well. If you do these exercises together, the resulting conversation will cause you to feel even closer in amazing ways.

Once you've done these exercises, you'll have more insight into the negative baggage you've been carrying around. And that's a good start. Now, it's time to take an even closer look at how that baggage affects the way you view the world and the people around you—including, but not limited to, the irrational people you're trying to reach.

While much is written in psychology about being happy with yourself, happiness is actually more closely tied to how you perceive and emotionally react to the events and people around you. That's because people who perceive the world as positive or negative will react to it positively or negatively.

If you perceive the people around you negatively, you'll react negatively toward them. And in return, they'll consciously or unconsciously change their own behavior, reacting more negatively toward you. For example, irritability begets irritability, and anger begets anger. It's a self-fulfilling prophecy. And so is the opposite: If you perceive people as loving, kind, caring, and trustworthy, they will be more likely to see you in the same way.

To see other people in the best light, and to allow them to see you in the best light, you need to explore your own worldview—and, if necessary, change it. That's what this final exercise is all about (see Figure 5–1).

FIGURE 5–1: Identifying Your Worldview

How do you generally perceive the world and the people around you? Take a piece of paper, and write the numbers 1 through 40 down one side (or photocopy this exercise). For each trait, decide where your feelings about other people land on the line between left and right. You can score your experience by giving each item a grade from A to F.

You may want to do a separate exercise for your family, your work, and your friends.

	LOW	F	D	C	B	A	HIGH	
1. Talking at								Talking to
2. Lecturing								Listening
3. Reacting								Thinking

	LOW	F	D	C	B	A	HIGH	
4. Impulsive								Thoughtful
5. Bored								Contemplative
6. Agitated								Relaxed
7. Excited								Joyful
8. Feeling empty								Feeling fulfilled
9. Frustrated								Satisfied
10. Busy								Productive
11. Ineffective								Effective
12. Disappointed								Grateful
13. Gloating								Gracious
14. Unforgiving								Forgiving
15. Mean								Kind
16. Exasperating								Inspiring
17. Taking								Giving
18. Ignoring people in need								Being helpful
19. Resentful								Loving
20. Laughing at								Laughing with
21. Judgmental								Open-minded
22. Impatient								Patient
23. Selfish								Generous
24. Blaming others								Taking responsibility
25. Having sex								Making love
26. Rushed and rough								Tender
27. Closed off								Open

	LOW	F	D	C	B	A	HIGH	
28. Artificial								Authentic
29. Unreliable								Reliable
30. Taking for granted								Cherishing
31. Negative								Positive
32. Pessimistic								Optimistic
33. Downbeat								Upbeat
34. Deflating								Uplifting
35. Apathetic								Passionate
36. Sluggish								Energetic
37. Passive								Active
38. Distrustful								Trustful
39. Untrustworthy								Trustworthy
40. Entitled								Deserving

Now look at your scores. Do you view the world and the people around you as more negative (closer to the left column) or more positive (closer to the right column)?

If most or all of your responses fall closer to the left, you're viewing things in an unhappy, resentful way—and that, in turn, will affect how you feel toward other people (including the ones you think of as crazy) and how they feel toward you.

If you want to change the way you perceive and react to the world, you may need to prime the pump of positivity. To do that, identify the negative qualities that you find most bothersome in the people around you and start acting toward these people as though they're exhibiting the opposing positive qualities. For example:

▶ If you think of the people around you as impatient and self-ish, envision them as patient and generous—and remember the kind things they've done for you.

▶ If you perceive the people around you as unreliable, think of them as reliable.

▶ If you perceive the people around you as unloving, picture them as loving.

What will happen when you do this? The people who truly are negative may come around, at least a little. And the people who aren't truly negative—the ones you've been misperceiving—will respond to your new behavior with relief, gratitude, and warmth. And occasionally, you may discover that the irrational person in the relationship was actually you.

I know that you may be eager to jump into talking to "crazy," and that all three of these exercises take time. However, they're crucial if you're trying to reach an irrational person. Otherwise, you're going to be playing defense the entire time.

And here's a huge bonus: You'll find that your negative thoughts influence not just your relationships with irrational people, but your relationships with everyone else—and the way you approach life overall. Neutralizing these thoughts will make you less crazy all around. And if that isn't successfully talking to "crazy," what is?

chapter 6

Keeping Your Own Crazy at Bay When You're Under Attack

IT'S CRITICAL to prepare yourself before you enter into a conversation with crazy, but all the preparation in the world won't help you if you fall apart once that conversation begins.

Confrontations with irrational people typically follow a predictable script. Unfortunately, it's a bad script. Here's how it goes: You decide that it's time to confront the person. You gather your courage. And you start talking. But a few words into the conversation, the person starts seething silently or tossing grenades like these:

"Maybe I'll just kill myself and make you happy."

"I know you've always hated me. Thanks for proving it."

"F#@& you."

"Go to hell."

"You're wrong."

"You've always disappointed me."

"You're an idiot."

"Get out of my face."

"You disgust me."

"I never want to see you again."

As the person escalates this attack, you get defensive. And then you get even more defensive. And then you get angry and scared.

Before you know it, you slide from defensiveness to irrationality. Stress hormones surge through your body, and your heart begins pounding wildly. You get flushed. You start shaking, yelling, cursing, or crying. Finally you think, "Never again," and walk away defeated.

So, what's the end result of your encounter? You feel humiliated, angry, sick to your stomach, and frightened because you lost control. You think, "I will not put myself in a situation like that again." If the person's attack was vicious enough, you may even believe, "I won't be able to survive another experience like that."

At the same time, the irrational person thinks, "I won."

Consequently, the irrational person gets even more locked into defending her unrealistic beliefs and gets even crazier. And that means you've made things worse, not better.

Now, here's what's really happening in this situation.

To you, the irrational person appears dangerously unpredictable. But in reality, irrational people will predictably escalate if you disagree with them, say no to them, tell them they're wrong, or ask them to do something they don't want to do.

When that happens, you, too, will react. And this means that you'll push back when the irrational person goes on the attack.

The difference is that you will escalate from a difference of opinion to a disagreement to the beginnings of an argument. At that point, still being relatively sane, you'll want to cut your losses and stop.

But that's not what the irrational person will do. As soon as a conversation turns into a difference of opinion, this person will rapidly (sometimes in a matter of seconds) escalate into a disagreement, then an argument, then a fight, and then all-out war.

Triangle/Silo/Triangle

To get a good grasp on why another person's crazy makes you crazy, think about the three brains we've talked about.

The irrational person's three brains start out like this, with the reptile brain in charge. This pulls the person toward fight or flight and also causes the person to see a narrow view of the world.

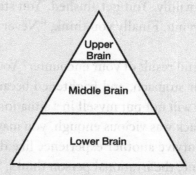

Your brain, on the other hand, starts out like this. Your upper brain is in charge, so you can think logically and see multiple viewpoints.

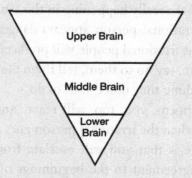

Even though you, too, may be a tiny bit crazy, your logical cortex is in control at this point.

As the irrational person pushes your buttons, however, your amygdala starts to send threat messages. As a result, your middle and lower brains begin to take more control. All three brains start vying for prominence, and your vision becomes increasingly constricted.

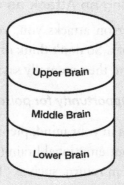

As you get more and more upset, your initial mature brain alignment flips, and your reptile brain takes total control, like so:

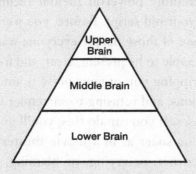

So at this point, both of you are coming from your reptile brains. For the irrational person, this is home turf, so he or she is just fine with it. In fact, the irrational person is totally comfortable going to extremes in order to push you into an amygdala hijack.

For you, however, being at the mercy of your reptile brain is terrifying. And that's why the other person wants to keep escalating, while you just want to escape.

In this scenario, the irrational person always wins and you always lose. At the same time, the irrational person also loses, becoming even more destructive or self-destructive.

How do you keep this bad script from playing out? By arming yourself with three weapons that can help you remain sane when crazy attacks you.

Weapon #1: Reframing an Attack as an Opportunity

When an irrational person attacks you, your instinct is to fight back. But that won't work. So don't think of it as an attack. Instead, reframe it by pausing and then mentally saying:

"Opportunity for poise."

To reinforce this idea in your mind, picture your cerebral cortex saying this phrase to your emotional brain (which may initially use some colorful language in return, such as "F#@& off, I don't want to be poised, I want to rip his throat out!"). Keep this conversation going in your mind until your cerebral cortex wins.

This is an incredibly powerful mental technique because it instantly rewrites your old script. Before, you were a victim. Now, suddenly, you're one of those people everyone wants to emulate—the people who are able to be present, clear, and focused under fire.

Remember: Stripping you of your poise is among an irrational person's best weapons, and refusing to surrender your poise is one of your best defenses. If you can do this, you'll go from being that minor character you sneer at in a movie theater—the one who's cowering in the corner, or crying, or blaming, or yelling—and transform yourself into the hero. That's the person who calmly handles zombies, vampires, or (in this case) everyday crazy without falling apart.

Again, say to yourself:

"Opportunity for poise."

Next, yell or swear at the person—in your mind, not out loud!—using whatever language you want to use. Then don't do anything. Just pause. And once again, think:

"Opportunity for poise."

If your amygdala is still champing at the bit, it may help to yell at *me* in your mind. For instance, say something like, "I don't care about poise right now, Mark, I want to throttle that no good %^&*#!" Then take a deep breath and repeat to yourself:

"Opportunity for poise."

Right now, the person you're talking with will be expecting you to get defensive and yell, start crying, or escape. When you don't, the person will be disarmed. And this is when you look the person squarely in the eye and say in a puzzled but not angry tone, "Whoa! What was *that* about?"

As you do this, watch closely. You'll notice that the person becomes upset because her verbal grenades didn't wound you. So she may say even more cruel and hurtful things.

If that happens, here's what you do: Simply repeat, "Yeah . . . and *that* too. What was *that* about?"

When you do this, you're likely to trigger a psychological response called an *extinction burst*. This happens when someone discovers that an old, reliable trick no longer works. Rather than giving up, the person will escalate the behavior to see if doing it more will work.

Let the person go off verbally on you again. Then say something like this:

> "I can't say I like your tone or style, but just so I don't miss the point you're making—what is it exactly that you'd like me to get from this?"

> "Not the best delivery on your part—but going forward, in your mind's eye, what exactly do you want me to start doing and what do you want me to stop doing, so we don't have this conversation again?"

Eventually, if you keep demonstrating poise, the person you're talking with will realize that lashing out wildly doesn't work anymore. At this point, you can steer the conversation back to more positive ground. And even if you still don't succeed in talking to "crazy" that day, you can feel proud of your own behavior.

One note: You may find it hard to keep your poise if you grew up with parents who went off the deep end every time they fought. If so, say to yourself:

"The more defensively I react, the more insecure I will look, and the more vulnerable to attack I will become. In addition, I'll be acting like my parents. And I don't want to model them."

Weapon #2: Picturing Your Mentors

Facing down crazy all on your own is a tough thing to do, but you don't need to be alone if you can call on the people you've looked to in your life as mentors. If you start feeling tense, think of your current or past mentors and supporters. Pause and take a deep breath. Then picture them beside you and think about what they'd advise you to say or do. This can give you an instant burst of wisdom and courage.

I have six deceased mentors, and in my mind's eye, I picture all of them supporting me as I go through stressful situations. As I do this, I feel a wave of gratitude toward them. I pause and let their love in, remind myself not to act on my impulses (which is advice they all gave me at one point or another), and then mentally thank them for making me stronger by believing so deeply in me.

Think of this approach as calling for mentor backup. Here's how to do it:

1. When an irrational person's arrows start hitting their mark and you feel yourself losing control, pause for a moment. If possible, say that you need to go to the bathroom or get a drink of water, so you can leave the situation for a moment. Otherwise, just don't say anything for a few minutes.

2. Once you've put your conversation on hold, think of two or more people who've loved and supported you. It doesn't matter whether or not they're alive.

3. Think of the reasons you're grateful to these people. Spend a few minutes feeling their love for you. Then imagine the advice they'd give you about your current situation.

4. Mentally thank your mentors. (If you're fortunate to still have them in your life, make a point to thank them for real later on.)

5. Rejoin the conversation.

One reason this approach works is that it's impossible to feel gratitude and anger simultaneously. When you allow gratitude to take over, you knock anger out. And that lets you return to your conversation with a clearer and more positive mindset.

The second reason it works is that even when your brain refuses to let you think clearly on your own, it can still call up sane advice from your mentors. And since that advice comes from people you love and respect, you're likely to follow it.

Weapon #3: The Eight-Step Pause

If you're talking to "crazy" and you sense that you're on the verge of falling into an amygdala hijack, you need to put the brakes on—and fast. Otherwise, you'll become just as irrational as the person you're trying to reach.

One of the best ways to stop an incipient amygdala hijack in its tracks is simply to pause. Pausing causes your amygdala to simmer down, allowing you to regain control of yourself and the situation.

The Eight-Step Pause is the best way I know to do this.

The Eight-Step Pause

STEP 1: Physical Awareness

Identify and pinpoint the physical sensations you're feeling right now.

Complete this sentence: "Right now I'm physically feeling _____
_____."

Fill in the blank with whatever physical sensation you're feeling (for instance, "a knot in my stomach" or "tension in my head").

STEP 2: Emotional Awareness

Attach an emotion to the physical sensation.

Complete the sentence: "And now I'm feeling _____
_____."

Fill in the blank with the emotion you're feeling, noting how intensely you're feeling it (for example, "very angry"), to completely capture your emotion in words.

STEP 3: Impulse Awareness

Put your impulse into words.

Complete this sentence: "This feeling makes me want to _____
_____."

Fill in the blank with your immediate emotional reaction (for example, "Tell my husband I hate him").

STEP 4: Consequence Awareness

Give yourself a reality check before you do something you'll regret.

Complete this sentence: "If I respond this way, what's likely to happen is _____."

Fill in the blank with all the possible consequences (for example, "I'll feel better for a moment and then feel guilty or embarrassed afterward").

STEP 5: Insight Awareness

Gain insight into the situation and your own response to it.

Complete this sentence: "Now that I'm a little calmer, I can see that I might be overreacting or taking the situation too personally in this way: _____."

Fill in the blank, identifying any misperceptions you might have (for example, you might say, "I took what my wife said far too personally, when she was just trying to point my attention to a behavior I really do need to correct").

STEP 6: Solution Awareness

Come up with a better solution than what you were going to impulsively do.

Complete this sentence: "A better thing to do would be _____
_____."

Fill in the blank with something that might work out better (for example, "to take a deep breath and agree with my wife, but tell her that I'll react better in the future if she doesn't use a scolding tone and I'd appreciate her trying to do that").

STEP 7: Benefit Awareness

Say to yourself what the benefit will be if you use that strategy.

Complete this sentence: "If I try that better strategy, the benefits will be _____."

Fill in the blank, listing as many benefits as possible (for example, "We won't get into an argument, my wife will feel validated, and I will feel more assertive about what I need from her").

STEP 8: "Let's Go" Awareness

Commit to taking action.

Fill in the blank: "Now that I did the first seven steps, what I am going to do is _____" (for example, "try what I came up with in Step 6 and not wait for another argument to tell my wife how to give me constructive criticism in the future").

If, like me, you aren't great at self-talk, imagine doing this exercise with someone who cares or cared about you. I picture my mentors going through the eight steps with me.

TIP

This also is a great exercise to do with teenage and even younger children because it helps them gain more control over their emotional reactivity.

When you do this with a child, you are actually teaching the child's mind to listen to her upper rational brain instead of being hijacked by the amygdala and thrown into her lower "fight-or-flight" brain.

Training Yourself to Be Saner

Staying in control during a conversation with an irrational person—or during any life crisis—is hard, especially at first. That's because you need to remain calm even as you're experiencing a nearly overwhelming urge to give in to anger or fear.

The three techniques I describe in this chapter will help you battle your natural fight-or-flight instinct. However, these techniques won't come naturally at first. In fact, you may find yourself resisting the urge to try them. That's especially true if your life experiences make it hard for you to change longstanding behaviors.

But if you're serious about successfully talking to "crazy," these three tools are game changers. So make an effort to practice them every day, especially right before you meet with an irrational person. Talking to "crazy" is an Olympic-level skill, and you'll be less likely to experience defeat if you exercise beforehand and develop some serious mental muscle.

chapter 7

Regrouping
When Crazy
Wins

TALKING TO "crazy" isn't easy, and even when you do it the
right way, it won't always work. Sometimes your attempt to reach
an irrational person will hit a brick wall. And sometimes it will blow
up in your face.

When that happens, there's a good chance you'll have a meltdown. You may find yourself thinking, "Oh God, I've made things
even worse. This is a disaster. I'm screwed."

At this point, there are two things you need to do. The first is to
calm yourself down in the initial moments following the disaster,
and the second is to keep yourself from doing something stupid if
you can't calm yourself down. Here's how to approach each step:

1. The "Oh F#@& to OK" Speed Drill

When a crisis rocks you, you need to move through five steps before
you can think clearly again. Unfortunately, it can take hours or days
to move through these steps. And in the meantime, you won't be
thinking straight—and you may say or do destructive things.

Fortunately, I've developed a way to fast-forward through this
recovery process so you can calm down in minutes instead of hours
or days. As a result, you can get yourself out of the danger zone fast.

If you're familiar with my book *Just Listen*, you know the drill I'm about to discuss (and thanks for bearing with me). If not, here's what to do in the moments following a disastrous confrontation with crazy.

The "Oh F#@& to OK" Speed Drill

"OH F#@&" (THE REACTION PHASE)

Do not deny that you're upset and afraid. Instead, identify your feelings and acknowledge them, silently using words to describe your feelings (for instance, "I'm really scared"). Say this out loud if you're alone, because the physical act of exhaling as you speak will help to calm you.

If you're able to get away for a minute or two, do so. If not, do not talk to anyone else during these first few seconds. You need to focus entirely on acknowledging and working up from your anger or panic. If you're able to keep your eyes closed for a minute or so, do it.

"OH GAWD" (THE RELEASE PHASE)

After you admit the powerful emotion you're feeling, breathe deeply and slowly through your nose with your eyes closed and let it go. Keep doing this as long as it takes to let it go. After you've released your emotions, keep breathing and r-e-l-a-x. This will allow you to begin to regain your inner balance.

"OH GEEZ" (THE RECENTERING PHASE)

Keep breathing and, with each breath, let yourself go from Defcon 1 back down to Defcon 2, 3, 4, and 5. It may help to say these words as you go through this transition: "Oh f#@&!" "Oh Gawd." "Oh geez . . ."

"OH WELL" (THE REFOCUSING PHASE)

Start to think of what you can do to control the damage and make the best of the situation.

"OK" (THE REENGAGING PHASE)
If you've had your eyes closed up to now, open them. Then do what you need to do.

Initially, this drill will be hard to do. That's because it's not instinctive for your brain to move instantly and fluidly from primitive to higher regions. It's far more instinctive to get stuck in "Oh f#@&" for minutes or hours.

So work at it. Do this drill whenever you experience a crisis at home or in the office. Over time, you'll find that you can gain control over your emotions more and more quickly. And when you do, you'll be able to move quickly from "Oh f#@&" to "OK" when an attempt to talk to crazy takes a bad turn.

2. The 72-Hour Rule

If you're lucky, the "Oh F#@& to OK" speed drill will help you regain your equilibrium after a talk with crazy goes wrong. But if not, you may experience an emotional breakdown. You may wind up in a blind panic, or feel like you're going crazy, or feel a powerful urge to lash out or do something self-destructive.

If you give in to your impulses during this time, you're going to do stupid things you will regret later. You may even do things you'll regret for years or for the rest of your life.

But here's the good news: Most breakdowns lead to breakthroughs. When I ask people who've had breakthroughs if these followed on the heels of breakdowns, close to 90 percent of people say yes. In other words, if you can do the right thing while you're melting down, you may come out of your ordeal with a new and better vision.

Fortunately, there's a simple secret to allowing a meltdown to make you stronger. I call it the 72-Hour Rule. The trick is to keep saying this to yourself: "This is a breakdown. I will survive it, and it usually leads to a breakthrough. So for 72 hours, I will not do anything to make it worse."

Of course, this is harder than it sounds. When you're in the middle of a breakdown, it feels awful, and in some cases it feels as if you won't survive or you are about to go crazy. The urge to do something is strong.

But don't.

If you're tempted to act, remember: 72 hours is the amount of time that psychiatrists can put patients on an involuntary hold, giving them time to calm down so they won't act on some dangerous impulse. And in the midst of your personal meltdown, that's how long you need to regain control.

Therefore, when you're experiencing a meltdown and feel like you need to do something right now, take the following actions. These will help you act maturely rather than making a bad situation worse. In essence, it's like giving yourself an adult time-out until you're sane again.

Step 1

Acknowledge that you're having a meltdown, and state (silently, or out loud if it's safe to do so) how you feel. Better yet, write down your feelings. Fill in these blanks in as much detail as possible:

_____

"I feel disappointed because _____."

"I feel frustrated because _____."

"I feel angry because _____."

"I feel afraid because _____."

"I feel hurt because _____."

"I feel self-doubt because _____."

"I feel guilty because _____."

"I feel ashamed because _____."

_____

Don't feel the need to justify anything you say or write. Just acknowledge your meltdown, say what you're feeling, and then feel it (instead of hiding from it, denying it, or blaming it on someone else). Remember that when you label your emotions accurately, it significantly lowers your emotional agitation.

If the pain from your meltdown still feels unbearable after you do this exercise, seek out a trusted friend or family member or a mental health professional to talk it out and talk it through. This will help you avoid doing anything to make the situation worse.

Step 2

Do this:

- Take a piece of paper and write down the exact time.

- Calculate what day and time it will be 72 hours later.

- If you have the urge to get drunk, binge on food, buy something you can't afford, or beat up on someone (either verbally or physically), tell yourself, "I have to wait until that time to do it."

This simple rule can spare you from a world of guilt, embarrassment, or shame. It can also prevent you from turning into the bad guy yourself in situations involving irrational people. And, as I mentioned near the beginning of this chapter, it can lead to a major breakthrough.

I can't prove my theory, but I believe that a breakdown loosens the connections between your thinking, emotional, and reptilian brains. This may explain why people having a meltdown often say they're becoming "unglued," "unhinged," or "wigged out."

My idea is that a meltdown occurs when the lens through which you view the world hits a new reality that isn't going to change. Initially, your mind is too rigid and brittle to adapt, and so it breaks down.

When this first happens, you may feel fragmented or shattered. But in reality, your three brains are already beginning to reconfigure and "mind see" the world differently. It's from this different "mind sight" that breakthroughs occur.

Apologizing to Crazy

If a conversation with crazy went south and you lost control, there's a good chance you said or did hurtful things. If so, then you owe the other person a sincere apology.

This will be tough on you—and I know it seems completely unfair, because from your point of view, the irrational person goaded you into having your meltdown. However, your apology will disarm the person and cause you to feel better about yourself.

So go up to the person and say, "I want to apologize for getting so defensive and being thin-skinned about what you said. I'm working on handling things better when people tell me something I don't want to hear." When you do this, it'll increase your chances of putting your bad encounter in the past and help you set the stage for a more successful conversation with crazy in the future. If you're lucky, it may also trigger a reciprocal response, making the person own up to his own role in derailing the conversation.

Of course, you'll need to be prepared for anything when you approach the person to apologize. Some people are simply unable to accept an apology, no matter how kindly it's delivered. (People with the personality disorders I discussed in Chapter 4, for instance, rarely handle an apology well.) If the person responds in a negative way, don't be discouraged. Realize that just because you apologize doesn't mean the other person can comprehend or accept it.

Most of the time, however, you'll make things far better when you say, "I'm sorry." And sometimes, as you'll see in this example, even when you think your apology failed, you'll be surprised later.

Mary, a middle-aged businesswoman, invited her colleague Laura to lunch in an attempt to help heal their troubled relationship. After setting the stage, Mary told Laura that she was sorry for her part in their falling-out. Then she offered Laura a single fresh red rose as a symbol of peace.

Laura simply stared at Mary coldly and refused to acknowledge her apology. Then she rose abruptly, said, "Good-bye," and left the restaurant.

Mary was used to getting the silent treatment from Laura, so fortunately she was well prepared for this strange encounter of the worst kind. Later she told me, "I feel freer and stronger. I did the right thing, and I did my best." She felt she'd risen above the occurrence and had seized an opportunity for poise.

And there's an interesting postscript to this story. A few months later, Mary told me that Laura had suddenly started talking with her again, as if their estrangement had never happened. Mary said it took all her strength not to start the discussion again and dig up the past—but she succeeded.

Be Willing to Try Again

If your conversation with crazy ends badly, you may be so shaken that you decide to avoid any more difficult conversations with the person you tried to reach. In fact, you may hesitate to interact with anyone who's acting crazy. If that's the case, realize that hiding from or surrendering to irrational people won't work. Instead, you'll just make things worse.

Research shows that avoiding touchy conversations comes at a high cost. One study by VitalSmarts Research, for instance, found that employees waste an average of $1,500 and one eight-hour workday for each crucial conversation they avoid. And on a personal level, avoiding sensitive conversations forces you to remain hostage to an irrational person's behavior forever.

So resist the urge to avoid or mollify the irrational person in your life. And don't give in to the temptation to call it quits if you lose a round or two in the "talking-to-crazy" game. Even professional therapists don't always come out of a session unscathed—but over time, we nearly always find a way to get through to our patients.

Instead of hiding, seek out the irrational person. Anticipate her crazy. When it happens, smile and say, "Here it comes." And then lean into it again.

SECTION 3

Fourteen Tactics for Talking to "Crazy"

Now that you know what makes people crazy—and how to handle your own crazy—you're ready to master my favorite "power tools" for handling the irrational people in your life.

These strategies range from gentle to confrontational to a little dangerous. When you're choosing a strategy, the person's M.O. and your own level of willingness to lean into the person's crazy will dictate your approach.

chapter 8

The Belly Roll

Putting the Irrational
Person "in Charge" to
Defuse a Tense Situation

IN CHAPTER 1, I said that when you talk to crazy, following your
own instincts usually won't work. Instead, you need to act counterintuitively. And to bring that point home, I'm starting this section
of the book with a strategy that's totally counterintuitive—especially
for men.

When you're talking with an irrational person, your natural
instinct is to try to take charge of the conversation. That's because
we typically think of dominating as winning and submitting as losing. And this is especially true for high-testosterone guys.

But if you try to dominate a person who's in attack mode, that
person is going to respond by going for your throat. You're both
likely to come away severely scarred, and the two of you are going
to remain enemies rather than finding common ground.

And here's something else to understand: Often, irrational people's worst behavior occurs when they feel powerless. Pushing back
at them in this situation will cause them to feel even more powerless
and inflame them.

Instead, try something noninstinctual. I call it assertive
submission.

I know that sounds like an oxymoron, but it isn't. To understand how assertive submission works, think about two dogs fighting. There are three ways this scenario can end:

▶ The dogs can fight until they're both seriously wounded.

▶ One dog can run away, sending the other dog into uncontrolled predator mode.

▶ One dog can roll onto its back, showing its belly to the other and basically saying, "I agree. You are the dominant dog. What do you want me to do?"

Now let's look at option three—the dog equivalent of assertive submission—and talk about how it works with people.

Remember the road-rage story I told back in Chapter 1? In that situation, I didn't argue or try to reason with the angry driver who wanted to kill me. And I didn't try to run away. Instead, I acknowledged that the man could kill me. And then I gave him permission to. In fact, I almost insisted on it.

If that's not assertive and submissive, I don't know what is.

So what happened when I did the human equivalent of a belly roll? First, I validated the man's dominant status (which I'd put in jeopardy by cutting him off as though he didn't matter). And second, I put my life in his hands.

When you lean into crazy in this way—by putting the irrational person in charge of you—you instantly change the relationship. That's because increasing the person's power lessens his need to act out. In a split second, you stop being a threat. Instead, in a sense, you become part of the other person's pack, under that person's domination. And that person will often respond, unconsciously, by wanting to protect you, because that's what pack leaders do.

That's exactly what happened in my road-rage incident, in which my assailant turned in a heartbeat from an attacker, screaming obscenities and pounding on my car, into a protector ("It'll be okay. Just relax"). And it's what will often happen if you try this yourself.

If you read my book *Just Listen*, you'll see that the Belly Roll has a little bit in common with the baring-your-neck technique I write about there. But when you bare your neck, you simply admit your weaknesses, which is fine when you're dealing with people who care about you and who are relatively sane. When you bare your belly, however, you go much further. That's because you admit your weakness and then neutralize the crazy by putting the irrational person in charge of what happens to you next.

I know this sounds like a dangerous thing to do, especially when the person you're dealing with doesn't have your interests at heart. However, it's amazing how well it can work. Here's an example.

Brian was a software developer for a major information technology (IT) firm. At 48, he'd been with the company for more than a decade and he'd taken the lead in developing several of its flagship products.

Now, however, he was working with a team of younger developers fresh out of college. These developers had strong opinions about how they wanted to update the company's products. From their point of view, Brian was a fossil. From his point of view, they were screwing up his software with unnecessary bells and whistles.

In meetings, the conversations often got ugly. Angry that they were altering his code in ways he didn't like, Brian would state his complaints forcefully. Because he was a big guy, he came across as belligerent and intimidating. The other developers would spiral into crazy in response, becoming emotional and hostile. Screaming matches frequently ensued.

At the time, Brian's wife was working on a project with me, and she happened to bring up Brian's issues. I suggested that the assertive submission approach might help, and I mentioned the analogy of the dogs.

When she got home that night, she told Brian about our conversation. Brian cut her off, saying, "I have a right to defend my opinions." But apparently he filed that dog story away somewhere in his unconscious mind.

A couple of weeks later, one of the younger developers suggested a major revision that Brian believed was unnecessary and would weaken the product. Once again, he went on the attack. And once again, the younger members of the team got their hackles up, raising their voices and in one case even pounding on the table.

And then, Brian paused. His conversation with his wife came back to him. And at that moment, he did something that, for him, was truly remarkable. "Okay," he said. "Let me say something here. I just realized that I'm a big guy, and when I yell, I can be kind of scary. I guess to you all, I come across as a pit bull. But from my point of view, I feel like a little Chihuahua. Also, I can't stand bullies, and I'm embarrassed because I realize that I'm acting like one.

"Right now," he continued, "I'm concerned about the changes we're making to our software, but I don't want to come across like a jerk or a bully. So tell me how you'd like me to approach this issue, and I'll do my best."

Instantly, the tension in the room dissipated. One of the young developers said, "Hey, man, we appreciate that." The other developers suggested ideas and compromises. And in the end, they came up with a plan that worked for everyone—even, pretty much, for Brian.

Interestingly, Brian's assertive submission had long-term effects. Before that point, the other developers had actively tried to avoid him. But now that they weren't his enemies, they began to realize that he had years of expertise and inside knowledge.

To the surprise of nearly everyone, Brian eventually became a mentor to several of the youngest developers.

Clearly, assertive submission takes some nerve—as well as some humility. But my clients have used it to get through to everyone from ex-spouses to business partners. And here's another interesting thing about this technique: Often, it works in a situation that I think of as institutional crazy.

Institutional crazy occurs when otherwise sane people are determined to follow an institution's rules even when the rules are irrational or destructive. If you work for a large corporation or a government agency—or if you need to deal with one of these institutions—this technique can help you break through to people who are completely trapped in this kind of bullying.

In fact, I once helped a client use this technique to survive someone just as scary as my road-rage guy, but scary in another way: an agent from the Internal Revenue Service (IRS).

One of my clients, Sally, was a dedicated social worker at a Veterans Affairs hospital who put her whole heart into helping her patients. But this time, she needed help herself.

The IRS was auditing Sally and wanted a massive amount of documentation from her. Sally confessed to me that she was extremely disorganized. She said that half of her receipts were barely readable, and most of the rest were lost.

The fact that she had to go to the IRS office for an audit had Sally in a panic. As a low-paid social worker, she was hardly in a place to hire a tax attorney. Besides, she confessed that she didn't know what an attorney would make of her mess.

Sally told me that she was allowed to bring one person with her to the IRS office, and she asked me if I would go with her. I knew she was already dealing with some very heavy issues in her life and wasn't in the right emotional state to sort through her paperwork, hire a tax attorney she couldn't afford, get a delay, and try to find her lost receipts. (This was back in the dark ages, when it was tough to track down old receipts.) So I agreed to accompany her.

Sally started to cry with relief. But I admit that at that moment, I had no idea what I was going to do.

A week later, I met Sally outside the IRS office on Olympic Boulevard in West Los Angeles. She was panicky, despite having taken an antianxiety medication I'd prescribed. We went up to the waiting room on the fourth floor: Sally, me, and her little shopping bag of sad, crumpled receipts.

Luckily, by then I had a strategy in mind.

As individuals, IRS agents are as kind and compassionate to their friends and family as anyone else. But on the job, as part of a demanding bureaucracy, they're indoctrinated to go on the attack—and to stay on the attack, even past the point of reason. And because they're dominant in any relationship with a taxpayer, they can get away with it.

In a few minutes, it was time for Sally's appointment. Not surprisingly, the first IRS agent we met with was unable to make much sense of Sally's bag of receipts. Within a few minutes, she said Sally would need to gather all the receipts the IRS demanded—something all three of us knew was impossible. In effect, the IRS agent was trapped in institutional crazy: "You need to do what you cannot do."

Before the agent finished talking, I could see Sally starting to lose control and hyperventilate. So I knew I needed to step in.

Turning to the agent, I said, "I have a confession to make. I am not a friend of Sally's. My name is Dr. Mark Goulston. I am her psychiatrist—and she is about to have a panic attack here."

As the agent stared at me curiously, I added, "Look, Sally helps veterans with major psychiatric problems who are facing some of the toughest challenges you can imagine. She's not a big, bad person trying to cheat the IRS; she is a wonderful person providing a life-saving service." Then I asked the agent to call in a supervisor.

The agent did, and explained the situation to her boss. After she finished, I could tell that her supervisor still believed that she had to stick to the rules. So on Sally's behalf, I did a Belly Roll.

"I agree that Sally is disorganized," I said, "and that she screwed up royally by failing to keep her receipts. She knows that it's her own fault that she didn't have the receipts and probably couldn't get them."

Then I said that Sally didn't know what to do. And I threw her on their mercy—in an assertive way. "Let's all sit down and sort through these receipts and Sally's disorganized notes," I said. "You can ask her whatever you want, and then you can come to what seems to be a fair estimate of a tax or penalty she should pay so you can get on to dealing with other people that the IRS is more interested in."

And believe it or not, it worked. After I finished speaking, the supervisor sat down and the four of us went through Sally's papers. In less than 45 minutes, we were done. And the supervisor concluded that if Sally would pay the IRS $900—a fifth of the amount she'd feared that they'd demand—the audit would be over.

As Sally and I left the office, I suspected that the IRS agent and her supervisor were as happy to put this incident behind them as we were. After all, I'd put them in the position of being alpha dogs. And that meant that psychologically, they needed to solve the problem in a way that protected both their jobs and Sally.

There you have it: A technique that, by making you appear submissive and seemingly weak, allows you to take charge of some pretty powerful people, including enraged drivers, belligerent coworkers, and IRS agents. How powerful is that?

Usable insight •

Sometimes you win the battle by surrendering.

Action Steps

If you're in a situation in which you're facing an attack and don't know what action to take, try one of these three versions of the Belly Roll. You can use these variations in person, over the phone, or even in an email.

Version 1: When you know you are in the wrong

Admit you are wrong.

Then ask, "What do you want me to do?"

Version 2: When you don't know what move to make

Say to the person, "If I say or do something, it will make things worse. If I don't say or do something, it will make things worse. Given that I have very little confidence in what to do now, I need you to tell me what you need me to say or do to make the situation better for you."

Then ask, "What would it take to make this right?"

Version 3: When you know you will need to say "no" to an unrealistic request

Say to the person, "I have to say 'no' to what you want, and I'm preparing myself for your reaction. I don't have any idea what your reaction might be. So I'm in your hands."

Then say, "Would you help me?"

• ▬▬▬▬

chapter 9

The A-E-U Technique

Highly Effective—But Scary

A-E-U STANDS for Apologize, Empathize, Uncover. It's an edgy (and slightly scary) way to cut crazy down to size.

This is not an approach I recommend if you're emotionally fragile, or if you're dealing with people who actively hate you and wish you harm. Even in the right circumstances, you need to use A-E-U with great caution. Think of it as the emotional equivalent of C4: highly explosive but brilliant for blowing up barriers.

One person who used A-E-U successfully was a middle-aged woman named Barbara. She'd contacted me because her family was in crisis and her marriage to her husband, Jeff, was breaking apart.

Barbara and Jeff's daughter, a divorced and highly unreliable parent, had three kids. One of them, at 14, was in a psychiatric hospital, having attempted suicide by slashing her wrists.

Caught up in her family's grief and turmoil, Barbara was almost always in a state of anxiety. But when she tried talking things out with Jeff, who had his own issues with his job, she'd work herself into hysteria. Jeff, overwhelmed, would turn away from her, rather than reach out. He acted out his crazy in a different way: by being controlling, shut down, and emotionally flat.

It was a chicken-and-egg situation. Did Barbara's onslaughts trigger Jeff to close down? Or did Jeff's stonewalling cause Barbara to go more off the rails? It probably won't surprise you to know that each of them wanted me to fix the other person.

Barbara came to my office first. At our initial meeting, she went on and on. As I listened, I said to myself, "She doesn't want any advice from me right now. She just wants to 'feel felt.'" That's because when you feel felt by another person, your distress becomes bearable.

It was easy for me to see what was going on between Barbara and Jeff. When your life is turned upside down, feeling alone makes it worse. Many people need to verbalize what they're feeling to someone who will listen and care. And when they spill out all the emotions they're feeling, it frequently results in that phenomenon I mentioned in Chapter 7: a breakdown that leads to a breakthrough.

However, people who are logical or withdrawn often respond to a torrent of emotions by pulling into a self-protective, armadillo-like shell. Sometimes they just need time to gather their thoughts. Other times, they feel emotionally battered by their partners' onslaughts.

If this situation happens again and again, everyone becomes crazy and everyone loses. The emotional person feels unheard and unloved, experiences an anxiety that escalates to near panic, and flails like a drowning person desperately grabbing on to a lifeguard. But the other person doesn't see it that way and instead becomes defensive or even disdainful. Once contempt sets in, there's little room for healing.

For Barbara and Jeff, things were becoming unbearable. The more she yelled and cried, the more he retreated. And the more he retreated, the angrier she became. They went from being lovers to being strangers, and they were well on the road to becoming enemies.

This was the state of Barbara and Jeff's relationship when she came to my office. I told her she needed to take action. "Right now, you and Jeff are at war," I said. "You need a way to defuse the situation." And I described the three steps of A-E-U.

The first step, I explained, is to apologize. That's because the best thing you can do when a relationship is falling apart is to say, "I'm sorry." Nearly any other approach will make the other person want to fight back or escape. But offering an unsolicited apology—something people almost never do—changes the dynamic instantly.

"What I'd like you to say to Jeff," I told Barbara, "either on your own or in a session with me, is: 'I need to apologize to you for something that I constantly do. When I get upset, it triggers a crazy part of me that can't stop talking or shut up. And what I don't realize at the time is that this overwhelms you and causes you to shut down. While I see that as rejection, you're just protecting yourself. I'm guessing that you're thinking, "Here she goes again."'

"Jeff will probably be dumbfounded," I continued. "He may even say some crappy things because he feels a little out of control in the conversation. That's because when you apologize without being abrasive, whiny, or controlling, you take control.

"Stay in control," I said. "And don't let anything he says push your buttons."

Next, I explained Step 2 of A-E-U: the empathy step.

I told Barbara to say something like, "I tried putting myself in your shoes, and I realized that being in control is critical to you. And right now, you don't feel in control—not in your job, not with our granddaughter, and most of all not with me. You are a person under siege. I never knew it was so bad, and to be really honest with you, I didn't want to know. And for that, I'm also sorry."

At this point, I explained, Jeff might not react—but he'd be taking it all in. He just wouldn't know quite what to do with this new Barbara.

And that, I told her, was the time for the next A-E-U step: uncover.

"This is where you bring out into the open the darkest thoughts Jeff may have about you—thoughts he might be terribly ashamed of," I explained. If she could let him off the hook for these, she might really break through to him.

It was time to light the fuse on the C4. I told Barbara to say this: "One final thing. I think at our worst times, you don't just resent me and want me to stop nagging. I think that at times you find me utterly repulsive and disgusting, hate me, and wish you'd never married me. I'm guessing that sometimes you'd like to get a divorce but you can't bear all the tumult that would cause. It wouldn't even surprise me if when I'm on a trip, you secretly wish I'd die in a plane crash, because then you'd be free without being the bad guy."

Barbara was stunned. "Whoa," she said. "That's pretty heavy."

"It is," I agreed. "And it's also true."

I explained that feelings like these are almost universal in marriages in which one person feels shut down and the other person seems to always be on the attack. Saying these things out loud takes away their horribleness and the shame the other person feels for thinking them.

"It's likely," I told Barbara, "that he'll reply with, 'Hey, I don't hate you or find you repulsive or any of the rest of that stuff. It's just that you make me nuts, and you're right—once you start going, you don't stop. And I just want to escape.'"

At that point, I told Barbara, "You can celebrate, because the war will be over. And you'll both win."

Barbara understood, and she agreed to try the A-E-U approach with Jeff and me in my office. She and I rehearsed the three steps: apologize, empathize, uncover. And after the third time, she said she actually liked the approach. "Our relationship doesn't seem so crazy now," she said. "It actually seems fixable."

"Good," I said. "Because next up is showtime!"

It played out almost exactly as I'd predicted, although Barbara still got the last word. After she apologized, empathized, and aired and accepted Jeff's secret thoughts, he expressed his respect and appreciation for what she'd just done. And then she added, "That's why I'm going to work on not going off the deep end so easily. It's not just for you. I need to do it for me."

Things got much better for Barbara and Jeff after that, and that's not the end of the story. Working together instead of against each other, they became a formidable team. They were able to begin healing their relationship with their daughter and to start dealing with *her* crazy. And with their combined support, their granddaughter was able to get her life back on track.

A-E-U is dangerous stuff, but often, it's worth the risk. And what's interesting about this technique is that it doesn't just work in drastic situations like Jeff and Barbara's. You can use it to handle just about any kind of crazy at work or at home. Here's how one friend of mine used it to handle an incendiary situation in her new neighborhood.

Recently, I talked with Michelle, a friend of mine who'd moved to Tennessee to retire and build a horse farm. While she'd always had a passion for the country life, she also had an LA-style in-your-face directness.

Michelle wound up moving next door to the Johnsons, who didn't have horses and didn't like them. The Johnsons' two adult children found Michelle's arrival particularly annoying because they liked to drive well above the 25-mile-an-hour speed limit on their road and often had to swerve to avoid Michelle on her horse.

To make matters worse, the Johnsons weren't that great about taking in their trash. On some windy days, their metal garbage can lids flew off and landed in the horses' lane. And those jagged-edged lids could severely cut a horse's legs.

Michelle brought up her concerns to the Johnsons, who just ignored her at first and then became defensive. Then things escalated when Michelle, who was used to the loud gossiping that always took place in Los Angeles beauty parlors, made the mistake of bad-mouthing the Johnson family in the town's only beauty parlor. When Mrs. Johnson heard about it, she was humiliated and furious. And when she and Michelle had a heated conversation, and Michelle told her she was overreacting—well, you can imagine how unpleasant things got.

Michelle realized that she'd gone too far, but she didn't know what to do. She told me over the phone, "They must really hate me, because they're very religious and this is the first year they didn't leave a holiday card in my mailbox."

"Would you like to fix the relationship?" I asked Michelle.

She paused and then said, "Yeah, I actually would, because the tension between us is really upsetting me."

I suggested A-E-U.

The first thing I told Michelle to do was to write the following letter and mail it to the Johnsons:

```
Dear Johnson Family,

I've given a lot of thought to our rocky rela-
tionship as neighbors and put myself in your
shoes and looked at my behavior, my horses,
and me. I didn't like what I saw. If you're
willing, I would like to come over and meet
with all of you at a time that is convenient
and apologize for a number of things and, if
you'll let me, make amends.

If there is "too much water under the bridge"
and you'd prefer to decline, I will respect
your answer. But I hope you won't.

Your carpetbagger neighbor from LA,
Michelle
```

The Johnsons reluctantly invited Michelle over. Facing them in their living room, she said exactly what I suggested:

"I want to apologize for what I said in the beauty parlor about your family. And please lay into me if you want. The fact that I come from Los Angeles and can have a big mouth, as many LA people do, is no excuse. When in Tennessee, I should do as the Tennesseans do. And unless you think I should leave well enough alone, I'm planning to go back to the beauty parlor and apologize for what I said behind your backs.

"Next, I want to apologize for giving you the one-finger LA salute when you drive close to my horse, which spooks her and me. Neither my horse nor I react very well to being spooked.

"Finally, I want to apologize for just being plain rude in a genteel Southern community. If I want people to obey the rules of the road, I need to obey the rules of the community around here."

Then, moving on to the "empathize" step, Michelle said:

"Next, when I put myself in your shoes, I realized that if I wasn't used to horses and I was used to driving at a certain speed, and suddenly a horse appeared, that would spook me and cause me to swerve my car. And I think that could cause me to get a little ticked off."

And finally, she lit the fuse with the uncover step:

"I realize that when we have run-ins, or when you hear my edgy voice or learn that I said something nasty at the beauty parlor, it could even drive you to wish that fat-assed woman and her fat-assed horses had never come here, would just go back where they belong, or even deserve to get run over by a truck. And I want you to know that I understand why you may feel that way."

When Michelle said all this, the mood in the room instantly changed. The Johnsons uncrossed their arms and relaxed their stiff expressions. They said they'd never wished for her or her horses to come to harm (although they unconsciously may have). And then they worked with Michelle to come up with ways to be more respectful toward one another.

The A-E-U technique is powerful in situations ranging from marital breakdowns to neighborhood feuds because even the most defensive people are defenseless against an apology, a display of empathy, and the relief of being cleansed of their dark thoughts. If you're willing to take a risk—and are brave enough to uncover your own ideas about what irrational people may be thinking about you—give it a shot.

Two cautions, however: First, carefully rehearse what you plan to say. And second, make sure you have your own crazy firmly under control before you open your mouth. You need to get A-E-U just right, because once you light that fuse, there's no going back.

Usable insight ●●●●●●●●●●●●●●●●●●●●●●●●●●●●

Many people are defenseless against an unsolicited apology because they've never received one.

Action Steps

1. Think of a difficult relationship you have with an irrational person and decide if you want to improve it. On paper, list the pros and cons of taking action.

2. If you decide you want to take action, put yourself in the other person's shoes and list some of the ways you make things difficult in the relationship.

3. Finally, write down some of the dark and deeply destructive thoughts this person might have toward you—thoughts he might feel ashamed of.

4. If you feel brave enough, try the A-E-U approach with this person. But be sure to write down what you plan to say and then rehearse out loud first. This is not an off-the-cuff technique.

●●

chapter 10

Time Travel

Getting an Irrational Person to Stop Dwelling on the Past and Focus Instead on the Future

I GOT THE IDEA for what I call the Time Travel technique from Marshall Goldsmith, a good friend and the author of *What Got You Here Won't Get You There*. Here's his advice: Rather than focusing on the past or the present, focus on the future you haven't messed up yet.

In other words, don't keep going round and round in the same tired conversation with an irrational person: "You never follow through." "You always undermine me." "You never take responsibility." "You've always let me down." Instead, visualize tomorrow or next year, or picture your lives a decade from now. And then help the person see into that future with you.

For instance, to an angry partner who's constantly venting at you, say, "I can tell that I'm doing or failing to do a lot of things, and this has upset you for a long time. Going forward, what in your mind's eye would you like me to do differently?"

If your partner says, "I need you to listen to me when I'm mad instead of blowing me off," agree that you'll do this. And then say something like, "Can I ask a favor? You don't need to agree to it, but I hope you will. Going forward, when I get home from work, could you let me know exactly what you need me to do, or not do, that evening—and tell me in a loving way so I won't feel like I'm under attack and want to escape?"

Time Travel is powerful when you're dealing with friends, partners, kids, and others you love. And it's a formidable preemptive move when you're dealing with extremely difficult or abusive clients. Here's how one of my clients used it to tame a pack of lawyers.

Gordon's company did IT consulting work for a group of litigation attorneys. Stressed from spending long hours with demanding clients, these lawyers often kicked the dog by screaming at Gordon and his staff whenever even minor problems arose.

Eventually it got so bad that no one in Gordon's office wanted to work with the lawyers. Gordon consulted me, and I told him what to do.

At his next meeting with the law firm's partners, Gordon said, "Going forward, in the event I have to tell you about an obstacle or setback, what is the best way to tell you? My other clients have told me things like, 'Don't do it by email,' 'Don't tell me on a Friday,' or 'Just spell out our options for getting back on track.' What works for you? I'd appreciate it if you can be as specific as possible."

After they listed their preferences, Gordon said, "This is much too important for me not to get exactly right." He repeated their remarks back to them, asked if he had them right, and waited to hear the partners say, "Yes." In this way, he ensured that they had a clear agreement and that the client's expectations had been spelled out during a neutral and calm time.

Later, when a server problem hit Gordon's team and delayed a project for a day, he called one of the partners. "I'm not sure if you remember a conversation we had about how best to communicate with you about bumps in the road," he said. "If memory serves, you gave me these guidelines." He repeated the guidelines. Then he said, "We've hit one of those bumps. So I'm following through exactly as you instructed me." And for the first time—remarkably—the lawyer responded civilly instead of going for Gordon's jugular.

One of my favorite things about the Time Travel strategy is that you can use it to deal with almost any kind of crazy, large or small. It's kind of a one-size-fits-all approach.

For instance, it works really well with the indecisive people in your life, those who tend to stop forward progress in its tracks, like the person who simply can't pick a restaurant when you want to go out to eat. In this situation, you can say, "Going forward, unless there's something I'm really craving, I'm going to ask you where you'd like to go out to eat. If you can't decide, I'll give you a little time. And if you still can't make up your mind, I'll pick a place and that's where we'll go. I'll do my best to pick a place you'll like, but I'm going to make the decision."

Also, try it on those Monday-morning quarterbacks who insist on beating up on you after you make a decision that doesn't work out, even though their comments do no good and instead trigger guilt and resentment in you. Here's what to say to them: "Going forward, after I make a decision, unless I ask for your input, I don't want you to tell me what I should have done differently. If you keep doing this, I'm going to stop telling you about decisions I've made. That's not because I want to be evasive. It's because I don't want you to chime in after the fact. However, I will sometimes ask for your input *before* I make decisions."

The Time Travel technique is flexible in another way: You can vary your power setting. Up to this point, I've talked about how to do it in a firm but friendly way. But there's also a nuclear option. Save this for when you want to make it absolutely clear that a behavior you tolerated in the past is unacceptable and is going to end.

In this case, you're not saying, "Going forward, here's what we can expect from each other." Instead, you're saying, "Going forward, this is what I will expect from you. Period."

The key here is not to talk, but to act. Words respond to words, and actions to actions. So when someone continually acts out, you need to decide what action you will take in return. This needs to be a nonnegotiable item.

When you formulate consequences for a person's crazy behavior, don't think of this as attacking or punishing the person. Instead, you're leaning into the crazy and essentially saying, "You can do this if you want, and I'm not going to argue with you or try to change your mind. But here's what's going to happen if you do."

For instance, if you have an overly emotional partner, say this: "Going forward, if you start yelling or slamming doors, I will not enter into a conversation with you. Additionally, I'm going to ask you to leave the house, take a drive, or maybe even stay in a hotel until you cool down. If you refuse, I'm going to have a bag packed, and I will leave."

To use the Time Travel strategy in a situation like this, spell out the consequences of a person's future actions. Here are the three steps:

1. Make a list of consequences for both positive and negative actions. Focus on behaviors and consequences that are specific and observable, so there is no room for misinterpretation. And make sure the consequences are realistic and will matter to the person.

2. After you outline the consequences, don't ask, "Do you understand what I've said?" Instead say, "What do you understand about what I've asked you—and why do you think what we're doing here is important?" This helps to make the person feel like a participant rather than a target.

3. If possible, have the person participate in setting consequences. This way, if he doesn't follow through, you'll feel more confident when you confront him.

I recommend putting Time Travel at the top of your list of strategies when you're dealing with an office dispute or trying to handle an irrational partner or child. And here's another scenario in which it's dynamite: when you're dealing with a bullying parent.

"You're not a bad daughter," I told Julia, a grown woman with children of her own.

Her body shook as she sobbed. Her 87-year-old mother, Berna, living in an upscale assisted-living facility, was in failing health. Although Berna was in better shape than most of the residents, she made everyone's life miserable. She complained incessantly about everything and bullied staff members until they dreaded caring for her.

Julia tried to be an advocate for her mother, but she found it increasingly difficult in the face of the woman's nastiness. Then there was Berna's constant criticism of Julia's children, who never called or visited. (Julia thought that they were merely doing what she would have liked to do—but couldn't.)

As a result, Julia found herself wishing that her mother would die.

The more she wished this, the guiltier she felt. And the guiltier she felt, the more she called and visited. If some animals attack when they smell fear, maybe it's the same with difficult parents who attack when they smell guilt.

Whatever the case, the more Julia tried to lessen her guilt, the more negative her mother became. And the vicious cycle was pushing Julia into a clinical depression.

I explained to her that many elderly parents would be appalled, but not surprised, to learn that their adult children wanted them to die. "And equally as many adult children would be relieved to know they aren't alone in feeling that way," I said.

Many middle-aged adult children live under a cloud that will not disappear until their parents pass away. For them, there is no such thing as good news—not when their mother or father is chronically ailing, and not when the parent is healthy but bitter or negative.

Watching a parent become weaker, sicker, or more enfeebled is stressful, of course. But most adult children can bear that. It's when that parent becomes vicious, hostile, and resistant to help that stress crosses over into distress. Then, the goal of assisting the parent in living the best life possible is replaced by the goal of relieving one's own suffering. And when an ailing parent like this gets a reprieve— for instance, when a doctor says, "Good news, his lung cancer is going into remission"—it's a cause for silent desperation over the prolonging of an intolerable situation rather than a cause for celebration.

The desire for a parent to die sooner rather than later can escalate into an obsession. At that point, it can take all of an adult child's energy to keep such a death wish from wreaking emotional havoc.

That was the threshold Julia found herself facing when she came to see me. How, she asked, could a good daughter think such awful thoughts, especially after the many things her mother had done for her and her family over the years?

I stressed that Julia's feelings didn't mean she didn't love her mother. Nor did they mean she really wanted her to die. They simply meant that she wanted resolution, to put this chapter behind her.

Furthermore, I told Julia that I thought she loved her mother deeply. But she couldn't love how her mother's negativity had so completely taken over her personality and reduced her to a bitter, angry shell of a person.

When Julia realized—not just intellectually, but also emotionally—that she did love her mother but resented her behavior, she felt emboldened to stand up to Berna in a new way. So she followed the steps I outlined for her.

On her next visit, Julia confronted Berna. "You're my mother, and I'm always going to love you," she said. "But going forward, if you continue to act as negatively as you are, I'm not going to like you. And if I don't like you, I'm going to visit you less often and shorten the amount of time I spend with you at each visit. What I will not do is let myself dislike you so much that I stop visiting altogether. Before I do that, I will shorten my visits to ten minutes per week and check in more often with the staff instead. I'm asking for your help in making the best of the situation, being respectful and kindly toward others, and showing the dignity that I know you are capable of."

Berna heard the resolve in Julia's words and did what bullies often do when called on their behavior in a firm, no-nonsense way: She listened. What's more, she changed for the better, and Julia was able to replace the death wish she'd been harboring with the true desire to visit her mom. She hadn't truly wanted her mother to die; she'd simply wanted to love Berna for the mother she once was, not resent her for the one she'd become.

This approach takes courage, but it often works rapidly. And surprisingly, irrational people are often highly relieved (secretly) to have clear boundaries set.

Remember Dina and Jack, the long-suffering daughter and bullied son-in-law of Lucia from Chapter 2? They plan to use the Time Travel technique. First, they're going to send Lucia off on a trip. Then Dina will call her and say, "Here is how I see things one month from now when you return home. Going forward, I will expect you to respect my husband and me. And I will expect you to appreciate the fact that we've opened our home to you. If you cannot do this, I will pack your belongings and find you a nursing home that will accept you. And if you refuse to enter the nursing home, or if you decide to leave it, I will not open my home to you again."

You may find it hard to use this nuclear option, even in extreme situations. However, it's often the best way to save a relationship—especially if that relationship reaches the point where you hate the other person and wish that she would die. And it's preferable to repeating an endless loop of old grievances.

So when you're sick of the past and feel trapped in the present, try moving people forward with the Time Travel technique. But whether you're using the soft-and-cuddly version or the nuclear option, I have one caution: Don't sabotage yourself. Follow through. Do exactly what you say you'll do. And don't do what you promise not to do.

Also, if you've had trouble with follow-through in the past, have a conversation with yourself that starts with these two words: "Going forward . . ."

Usable insight ••••••••••••••••••••••••••

Sometimes you have to divorce your past and marry your future.

Action Steps

1. If you're in a loving relationship in which you both act crazy at times, have a Going Forward conversation. First, ask what you can do to improve the relationship going forward. Then gently spell out how the other person could improve the relationship going forward.

2. If you're being battered by someone's unacceptable behavior at home or at work, use the nuclear option of the Time Travel technique. Lay out consequences for the person's future behavior. (If possible, involve the person in setting consequences. Otherwise, set them unilaterally.) Then follow through.

3. If you're a boss dealing with an irrational employee, use the Time Travel technique as you're coaching. Make sure you document the entire discussion for follow-up and reinforcement.

•••••••••••••••••••••••••••••••••• ▬▬

chapter 11

The Eye of
the Hurricane

Finding the Sane
Inside the Crazy

WHEN YOU'RE dealing with an irrational person, all you can see is the crazy: the screaming, crying, stony withdrawal, or lashing out.

But here's a secret: No one is totally crazy. Somewhere inside every storm is an area of calm. And when you're talking to someone who's over the top emotionally, one of the most effective strategies is to aim for that eye of the hurricane.

Decades ago, I was moonlighting on weekends at a state psychiatric hospital. One night, a schizophrenic patient named John went wild in one of the units, throwing all the chairs and tables around and smashing the television set in the day room. When I arrived on the scene, the three nurses were huddled in their station behind shatterproof glass. They'd called me to give an order for hard restraints and to inject John with an antipsychotic drug.

Directly ahead, with his back to me, I saw a huge man standing in the middle of the day room that he'd just wrecked. As I started toward him, the head nurse opened the nurses' station door and whispered loudly, "Hey! What are you doing? Wait until the techs get here to put him in restraints!"

"It's okay," I replied, "I'm going to go talk to him."

"You're crazy," said the nurse. And I suspected that she might be right.

When I got about 10 feet away from the patient, I called out to him: "Hey there, John!"

Startled, he turned around to look at me. "What?"

"I've got a question for you," I said. "Do you think there are any Camels in the cigarette machines in the hall outside?"

Smoking was the favorite day room activity. And Camel unfiltered was the brand of choice for nearly every patient.

John paused. He looked at me and said, "I don't know. Probably."

"Do you think they have matches in the machine?" I asked him.

He looked at me blankly. Then he laughed and said, "What, are you crazy? This is a mental hospital!"

I grinned and said, "You know, a nurse just called me crazy, too. And you're probably right about the matches. Anyway, I see that you've been kind of busy making a mess of this place, and you look tired. You also know the routine here. A few psych techs are coming in and will need to put you in restraints for a short while. As for me, I'm gonna go out and get some Camels. I'll come back in to give you one, and save the rest of the pack for you at the nursing station. Then I'll stay here to make sure things run smoothly. You okay with that?"

John looked at me almost sheepishly. "Yeah. I know I messed up."

"Hey, man," I said, "cut yourself some slack. You're in a mental hospital—you're not exactly expected to act normal. It'll be okay. Just try to relax."

And he did. We sat and talked casually about stuff—the ward, the nurses, cigarettes—just like everything was fine. Soon enough, everything *was* fine, and we could wave the psych techs away.

How was I able to reach John so quickly? By recognizing what the sane part of him—the calm part hidden under the rampaging, furniture-throwing, TV-breaking surface—really needed at that moment. In John's case, it was clear that he needed to find a road back to normal life as he knew it: a smoke, a friendly companion, and some casual gossip about the nurses. And that's exactly what I gave him.

Similarly, many people in the grip of garden-variety crazy—especially if they're normally pretty sane—are actually looking for a quick way out. So help them find it.

Finding the sane inside a person's crazy won't always be easy, and it won't come instinctively. That's because when you're talking to emotional people, your own hardwired response might be to:

- Shut down (which will only make them yell longer, because they'll think you're not listening).

- Tell them to calm down (which will only make them more upset).

- Try to point out how irrational their behavior is (which they will perceive as patronizing).

Don't do any of these things. Just let the hurricane blow. And instead of feeling pummeled by it, imagine that the storm is passing around you, and you're looking for the calm eye.

As the person vents, keep your expression empathetic and interested. Let him finish venting. And when the screaming or crying winds down, help him tell you what he needs from you.

TIP

When you're talking with someone who's highly emotional, focus on the person's left eye. I believe this trick works because the left eye is connected to the right brain. Just as the layers of your brain differ, so do the right and left sides. The right side is the more emotional side of the brain, which is where a screaming, crying person is coming from—so putting your attention there will help you connect with the person. More important, it will give you something to focus on other than the person's ranting.

Getting the person to tell you this will take a little work. One of the best ways to do it is to say, "I can see you're really frustrated. To make sure I don't add to your frustration, and to make sure I don't miss something, what do I need to do right now? What is the critical thing I need to do in the short term? And what is the most important thing I need to do in the long term?"

By reframing the conversation this way after the person stops venting, you invite his logical brain to kick in. If you succeed, you'll both wind up standing in the eye of the hurricane. And when that happens, you can talk about what the person really needs—and about better ways to communicate with you in the future.

Now, all of this sounds pretty simple. And it is—but there's a trick involved: You must fully believe that the person you're dealing with is sane on some level, no matter what he is doing or saying during a tirade. If you do not believe this, you will not succeed.

So instead of thinking of the person as crazy all over, think of him as partially crazy and partially sane. It's your job to get past the crazy and find the sane that you are absolutely sure is there. Once you do that, you can address the irrational person's needs and your own.

Here's another example of how it's done.

Kimberly had only one emotional setting: hysteria. She drove everyone at work crazy, and most of her coworkers dealt with her by avoiding her.

Jason, her manager, thought about firing her, but he knew that she had the potential to do excellent work, and he wasn't quite willing to give up on her. He was sure that somehow he could find a way to calm her down.

One day, Kimberly went ballistic about her workload. Her voice rising to ear-bleed levels, she shrieked, "Nobody realizes how much I already have on my plate. I can't believe you think I'll be able to get this done. You know how much I'm already handling, and you want the quality to be top-notch. Well, you can't have your cake and eat it, too, and you might have a nervous breakdown on your hands soon."

"Maybe I'm the crazy one, and maybe everyone else is right," Jason told me. "Maybe I should cut her loose. I don't know why I keep giving her chance after chance. I guess it's because in the end she does do good work, and I just don't think she can help herself."

Questioning Jason carefully, I established that Kimberly didn't have any major mental problems. "She's just a pain in the ass," he concluded.

I told Jason that the next time Kimberly came screaming into his office, he should let her vent. But as she did, he should focus on fully believing two things: that Kimberly had the ability to think clearly and that she had a logical need hidden somewhere inside her venting.

Even without meeting Kimberly, I told Jason that one of her logical needs was to have someone listen to her so she could get things off her chest. That's one thing all venters want, although ironically, their behavior stops people from listening. So that's the sane spot that Jason aimed for the next time she stormed into his office.

Jason let Kimberly vent. When she finally ran out of steam, he paused. And then he said, firmly but with sincere interest, "I hear what you're saying, and I can see that you're very upset. Can I ask you a question? What is the result that you want from our conversation? What specifically do you want me to do now, tomorrow, or in the future as a result of what you just said?"

Jason's remark made Kimberly pause. In a less angry tone of voice, she replied, "I want you to understand how stressed I am and stop overloading me with work."

Jason replied calmly, "Okay, that's pretty clear." Then, still in a sincere and truly interested tone, he said, "And I'm listening to what you have to say. But do you honestly believe that how you just spoke to me is going to get you the result you want? And even if it does, do you think it's going to make me want to be sympathetic to your situation?"

When he said this, Jason could see Kimberly's logical brain engaging even more. However, she wasn't quite ready to be rational yet. So she said in an aggrieved tone, "You're not helping me figure out how to get this all done!"

Jason replied, "I promise that I will help you. And I promise that I will listen carefully to everything you have to tell me. But I need you to ask for my help instead of screaming. When you scream, the last thing I want to do is help. But if you ask for my help, it's the first thing I'll want to do."

Then he waited.

And to his astonishment, Kimberly began to cry.

Jason, fearing that he'd made things worse, asked, "What's the matter now?"

Kimberly said, "I think I've always screamed because I never felt anyone ever listened to me. But you just took the time to try to understand, and that meant you actually felt I was worth listening to and worth understanding. That's something I've never experienced, and it's a little overwhelming!"

"The bad kind of overwhelming, or the good kind?" asked Jason.

Kimberly smiled through her tears. "Definitely the good kind."

Like Kimberly—and like John, the rampaging mental patient—many people feel that acting out emotionally is the only way to get their needs met. So they yell, sulk, cry, scream obscenities, or even lash out physically.

Most people react to this by retreating or shutting down. This leaves the irrational person thinking, "Nobody cares! Nobody listens!" As a result, the person decides that the only way to get through is to be more emotional the next time. That's why the yelling, screaming, sulking, or door-slamming keeps escalating.

When you do the opposite, by willingly leaning into people's emotional storms and finding the quiet eye within, you change this dynamic. That's because you show these people that they can be calm *and* get their needs satisfied.

"Too Much Crying"

After I finished the first draft of this book, I asked a CEO and friend of mine to read it. When I asked for his opinion, he said, "It's excellent, Mark. It's already helped me get through to two 'impossible' people. But there's just one thing: There's too much crying."

I laughed, because I totally understood where he was coming from. In several chapters, I talk about letting people cry or even encouraging them to cry. And to paraphrase Tom Hanks's character in *A League of Their Own*, most professionals believe that there's no crying in business.

I understand that one of the last things you want to do, especially at work, is deal with tears—and that's particularly true if you're a manager or CEO. After all, it's your job to plan projects, get results, and watch the bottom line—not to be a nanny or a shrink.

But here's the deal: If you learn to let people cry, and calmly observe what happens, you'll see that their outbursts typically lead them to a calm place where you can reason with them.

Think of crying as a high colonic: It happens because people desperately need to get something out, and in this case, it's tears. Generally, people need to cry so they won't do something worse—like act out physically or say, "I quit," or, "I hate you." Once they've drained their negative feelings, positive ones will usually rush in. And that's when the best conversations start.

If you're in this situation, think back to the advice I gave you in Chapter 6: Don't get embarrassed and don't run away; instead, say, "This is an opportunity for poise." And then exhibit it.

Do be aware, however, that this approach won't change emotional people's ingrained behavior overnight. Emotional craziness is a powerful habit that takes time to break. But if you can guide emotional people to that sweet spot of calm over and over again, they may eventually learn how to start from there themselves.

Usable insight ●

The first step in finding the sane inside the crazy is to believe it's there.

Action Steps

1. Think of someone in your life who frequently cries, screams, yells, slams doors, or otherwise acts out emotionally.

2. The next time the person flies off the handle:

   ▶ Let the person vent.

   ▶ Listen calmly and do nothing.

   ▶ If you are on the phone, resist the urge to hang up.

   ▶ If you are talking in person, focus on the person's left eye so you can connect with the person's emotional right brain.

3. When the venting stops, guide the person to the eye of the hurricane by asking:

   ▶ "What do I need to do right now?"

   ▶ "What is the critical thing I need to do in the short term?"

   ▶ "What is the most important thing I need to do in the long term?"

● ●

chapter 12

Digging Down to Disappointment

Dealing with Emotional People Who Don't Really Mean What They're Saying

WHAT I'M about to say may sound sexist. But hear me out, and maybe you'll forgive me.

In most couples, one person often appears more logical—not to be confused with less crazy, but more on that later—and the other more emotional. Usually, the person who appears more logical is the man, while the person who appears more emotional is the woman.

Obviously, this isn't always the case. But in three decades of working with couples, it's a pattern I typically see.

So I'm not surprised when I wind up with a man sitting in my office with his mouth set in a grim line while a woman screams at him, "You're just like my father!" or "You never loved me!" I'm not surprised when the man attempts to refute her arguments with logic, only to make her crazier. And I'm not surprised when once in a while the man simply gets up from his chair, says something like, "It's over between us," and walks out.

Here's something I know about this situation after years of watching it play out. The woman looks like the irrational person in the relationship. But often, the man is crazier.

Of course, this scenario doesn't always involve a man and a woman. In fact, here's an example of a father and son.

Bill, a man in his 30s, was sad about how distant his father, Sam, had acted for the past 15 years. When I asked Bill why he thought his father was distant, he said, "I have no idea."

A week later, I saw the two of them together. At that meeting, Sam told me about a day when his son, high on drugs at age 19, had told him, "I hate you! You're the worst father anyone I know has, and I wish either you or I were dead." Sam responded by backing away and keeping an emotional distance from his son that lasted from that day to the day they met in my office.

When he heard this story, Bill was stunned. He barely remembered the episode, because he'd been so high at the time. He shook his head and asked his father what that incident had to do with the gulf between them.

Sam said to his son in a calm and matter-of-fact way, "You were so clear about how much you hated me and wanted me away from you—even to the point of wishing either of us were dead—that I wanted to give you some space so it wouldn't get worse. And I guess that all this time, I was waiting for you to invite me back into your life."

Bill started crying. "But I was out of my mind on drugs," he said.

Sam became a little tearful with longstanding pain, saying, "I just thought that you really hated me and didn't want anything to do with me."

Now, here's the question: Who was the irrational person in this scenario? The answer: both of them. It's just that they were crazy in very different ways. And the person I want to focus on in this chapter is Sam, the seemingly rational one.

When people are emotional, they often say or do things before they think. Practically all of their crazy statements—which sound sincere in the middle of their tirades—are meaningless. Often, as in Bill's case, they don't even remember these statements.

Unfortunately, overly logical people like Sam don't get this. Their own M.O. is to think before they speak or act. And they think—mistakenly—that the other person is doing the same thing. This explains why when a logical person like Sam hears an emotional person say, "Get out!" or "I want a divorce!" or "I never want to speak to you again," the logical person begins to make plans to move out physically or check out emotionally.

And that's exactly what happened with Sam. Rather than digging down to uncover Bill's actual feelings, Sam went for an emotional checkout, leading to 15 years of lost time that he and his son will never get back.

In this case, logic isn't really rational. Instead, it's crazy—and that's why if you're the logical one, you need to do something different: Dig down to the emotion the person is truly feeling.

Here's how.

First, when you're faced with an emotional person who's saying wild things like, "You're a jerk!" or "I'm leaving," understand this:

The person doesn't mean it.

Why is the person saying it? Because she is simply overwhelmed by emotion at this point and needs to vent. While it may be hard for you to avoid reacting to the person's words, you need to realize that you can't take them literally.

To understand why, think of a soda. Normally, if you pop it open, it fizzes a little. That's the person on a normal day. But shake it up hard and then pop the top, and it'll explode. And that's what's happening in your situation right now.

So let the person continue to vent some more. Think of this as letting the foam pour out of a shaken soda can. And then, once the person starts to become calmer, dig down.

To do this, look into the person's eyes and say something such as, "I can see that you're really angry at me. Tell me: Do you hate me, or are you just incredibly disappointed in me for doing X (or failing to do X)?"

This will be extraordinarily hard for you to say at this point. After all, right now, in your universe, you're the rational person, and the emotional person is the crazy one.

But do it anyway. Because it's magic.

Why? In reality, the emotion that most often lies at the core of anger and venting isn't hatred or repulsion. It's disappointment. However, people rarely use that word. Instead, they use horrible, hateful words that they don't really mean.

When you offer disappointment to them as a choice, and they agree that they're disappointed rather than filled with hate, they often de-escalate quickly. And you become less defensive, too, because disappointment involves something you did—not the person you are at your core.

If the irrational person agrees—"Yes, I'm disappointed in you"—say calmly and empathetically, "How disappointed?" Then let the person talk some more. After that, dig even deeper and say, "What one thing have I done or failed to do that has most disappointed you since we've known each other?" And then apologize for it.

As hard as this may be for you, you'll see that it makes the person look at you in a different and kinder way. And another interesting thing is likely to happen: The person may turn to you and say something like, "I know I do things that disappoint you, too." And that can start a whole new conversation.

Now again, this all may seem completely unfair. You're not the one who's screaming. You're not the one who's weeping. You're not the one who's saying terrible, terrible things.

But what I usually discover when clients do the emotional-versus-logical dance in my office is that at some point, the logical person has knowingly or unknowingly deeply injured the emotional person by being cold, condescending, scolding, dismissive, or derisive (because that's how logical people typically respond when they're at their worst). That means both parties are at fault, and both parties should apologize.

I'm just asking you to go first.

Usable insight   •••••••••••••••••••••••

Just because someone is logical doesn't mean they're rational.

Action Steps

1. If you're dealing with a person who says wild things when she's emotional, tell yourself, "This person doesn't really mean it."

2. The next time the person becomes emotional, listen with your eyes, not with your ears. And once she has had a chance to vent, ask, "Do you really hate me, or have I just deeply disappointed you?" Then take it from there.

3. One caution: A person who is constantly emotional or enraged may have a personality disorder (see Chapter 4). If you believe that this is the case, seek professional help rather than trying this strategy.

•••••••••••••••••••••••••••••••••

chapter 13

The Fishbowl

Bringing an Irrational Person's
Mirror Neurons into Play

ANGRY OR hysterical people don't bother me. Neither do bullies. And neither do silent types, because it's easy for me to crack their shells and get them to open up. My own M.O. is to sit and listen calmly while these people talk their way back to sanity by openly venting their emotions.

Sometimes, however, I break with my M.O. and knock people out of their craziness by getting them to *stop* talking. Instead, I force them to speak with their eyes.

This approach, which I call the Fishbowl, harnesses the power of what I call mirror neurons. These brain cells fire both when you act and when you witness another person acting. And when another person is hurt or sad, these cells allow you to mirror the pain or sadness as if you're experiencing it yourself. V. S. Ramachandran, a pioneer in mirror neuron research, calls them empathy neurons.

When you ramp up the power of these mirror neurons, it's easier to get through to the irrational people in your life. Here's an example.

"I'm sorry, I just can't stop crying," Rick, a sales manager at a Fortune 100 company, told me as his boss, Jim, looked on.

The company had called me in to work with Rick and Jim because the rift between the two of them was threatening their division's success. Things reached a climax when Jim yelled at Rick in a team meeting, "I don't even know why I bother with you! You are an utterly useless human being!"

Rick was shaken and abruptly stood up to leave the room—whereupon Jim yelled out to him, "Useless and a coward to boot!"

The rest of the team was speechless. Most of them averted their eyes. Afterward, team members huddled in corners to talk about the incident. In the days that followed, the team felt awkward and uncomfortable around either Rick or Jim.

When I arrived a few weeks later, I sat down with Jim first, so I could hear his side of the story. He revealed that his own boss kept pressuring him to substantially increase his numbers, and he felt he needed to wake up his team. Jim's stress level was already sky-high when the meeting began, and Rick had unwittingly set him off by failing to have an answer for a question Jim asked him.

Next, I sat down with Rick. He told me that Jim was a bully who had it in for him, and that whenever Jim spoke to him in an abusive tone it triggered such stress that his mind would go blank.

After meeting with each of them alone, I sat down with both of them together. I began by using a strategy called the empathy jolt. The crux is this: You can't be sincerely empathic toward and angry with someone at the same moment.

I asked Jim, "If I were to ask Rick what caused him to get up and leave the room when you berated him in front of your team, what would he say?"

Jim was a little confused by my question. I tried again. "Put yourself in Rick's shoes at the moment he left that meeting. Now tell me what you think he was feeling."

With some contrition and embarrassment, he replied, "I think he felt beaten up by the schoolyard bully"—he gulped—"and that bully was me." Rick was obviously moved and even became a little emotional at Jim's admission.

I then asked Rick, "If I were to ask Jim what was going on with him at the moment he yelled at you, what would he say?"

Rick paused. Then he replied, "I think he would say he's under huge pressure to get our numbers up, and it's stressing him out."

As Rick spoke, I could see Jim becoming a little calmer and less hostile. We went on like this for some time, until I sensed that Rick and Jim might be ready to let go of their mutual dislike.

That's when I had them do the Fishbowl exercise. First, I asked the two of them to sit face-to-face, not saying anything. Then I asked them to look into each other's eyes and focus only on each other's eyes—not on me, not on the room, not on anything but each other's eyes.

Like most people, Jim and Rick began this exercise sitting stiff as boards, embarrassed and tense. But as the minutes ticked by, I could see them gradually relax their rigid postures and scowls. In fact, I even saw a few twitches that looked like the beginnings of smiles.

Once they were in this zone, I asked Jim to say to Rick, "I'm sorry about bullying and humiliating you in that meeting. And I am sorry about all the other times I've done it to you."

And then I asked him to say, "I was wrong."

At that point, Rick became overwhelmed with emotion. He began to cry, and couldn't regain his composure. This time it was Jim who had to avert his eyes.

When the raw emotion had run its course, I asked Rick, "What was that all about?"

He looked at me with red eyes. "I've never been apologized to in my entire life—much less had someone tell me that they were wrong for doing something hurtful to me."

And then he said to Jim, "Thank you."

.That knocked both Jim and me over. And it changed how Jim
and Rick acted toward each other from that day forward.

I call this exercise the Fishbowl because when people look deeply
and silently into each other's eyes, it's as if they're in a fishbowl that
excludes everything and everyone else. At first, this feels far too
intense and intimate, and people resist. But gradually, their harsh-
ness and contempt dissipate, and even hard-core enemies begin to
feel empathy toward each other.

This transformation occurs because when two people shut out
the entire world and look into each other's eyes, it sends their mirror neurons into hyperdrive. Since both people feel vulnerable,
they feel each other's vulnerability—and as a result, they drop their
own defenses. In effect, they get a glimpse into each other's souls.
And what they generally see is that the other person isn't a jerk or a
bully or a loser, but just someone who's scared or insecure or frustrated. That's why Jim was ready to apologize after doing the Fishbowl exercise, and it's why Rick responded with such deep emotion
to Jim's apology.

You can try the Fishbowl approach yourself in a personal relationship. In a business situation, I recommend having a coach or
trainer facilitate. Here are the steps of this approach:

1. Assume that the other person is truly good at heart and is
   doing the best he can. Believing this will allow you to see
   that the person, no matter how irrational, doesn't mean you
   harm—and this insight, in turn, will inoculate you against
   an amygdala hijack.

2. Tell the other person that you want to start by simply looking into his eyes, without talking. Be aware that he may be
   uncomfortable or resist at first. If so, just say, "I know this
   may feel awkward, but it will help me stay focused because I
   want to make sure that I get what you're feeling and understand what really matters to you."

3. Look deeply into the person's eyes, holding your gaze steady. As I've mentioned, I prefer to focus more on the left eye because I believe that the left eye is connected more directly to the right (emotional) brain. As you gaze into the person's eyes, fully believe that there is a great deal going on beneath the surface and that you want to find out what it is.

4. Once you feel that you're both "in the fishbowl," start a conversation as you continue to gaze into each other's eyes. As always, let the other person vent without becoming defensive or launching a counterattack. Also, use conversation deepeners such as, "Can you tell me more about that?" or, "What's really going on?" Finally, talk about what needs to change for both of you going forward.

One of the most remarkable things about the Fishbowl is how quickly it can move even highly resistant people from "I don't want to talk about it" to "I want and need to talk about it." I used this approach to get through to my own difficult-to-reach father when he was in the early stages of Alzheimer's disease. I use it today with angry couples and warring business partners who haven't spoken to each other for months. (You'll even find an example on YouTube of me using it on the talk show *Gabrielle*, if you search on my name and the term *marital hypnosis*.) And a friend of mine used his version of the Fishbowl to get through to some of the most tough and tight-lipped people on the planet: U.S. Marines.

My good friend Lt. Gen. Marty Steele, former U.S. Marine Corps chief operating officer and currently the executive director of USF Military Partnerships at the University of South Florida, is a master at reaching into people's souls by looking into their eyes. From 2006 through 2008, he spearheaded a transition program for marines returning from combat. In that one-week program, the marines received a great deal of assistance in preparing for life back in the civilian world. But hands down, what they found most life changing—and in some cases even life saving—were the 90 minutes they got to spend one-on-one with General Steele.

When I asked General Steele what he spoke to them about, he said he looked deeply into the eyes of these courageous and noble people. And then he kept repeating, "Marine, what's going on?" and then, "What's really going on?"

He told me that he just kept repeating it "until they spoke from their hearts and deeply troubled souls. And within a short time, they went from talking about some marital issue or job-related problem to saying something like, 'Sir, I saw and did horrible, horrible things.'"

I asked General Steele what he said next. "I told them that war is necessary," he said, "but it is not pretty, and that all marines who have seen active duty have seen and done some horrible things in the defense of freedom. I then told them that they needed to now put that aside and focus on their families and their lives and get back to building a happy and successful civilian life, because they so deserved it."

General Steele is a humble person, but I know for a fact that he's received many letters from marines and their families describing how those eye-to-eye meetings saved lives. Semper Fi to you, General Steele.

Usable insight ························

When you look into people's eyes with the sole purpose of understanding them instead of judging or maneuvering them, they no longer have a reason to keep their guard up.

Action Steps

1. If you're having trouble reaching an irrational person, acknowledge that the person is doing his best—even if it doesn't look that way from your point of view.

2. Tell the person that you want to try something new to help you focus on what he truly feels and needs.

3. Then tell the person that you are going to look into his eyes and that you want him to look into yours. You will feel your own empathy grow. Watch for signs that the other person is lowering his guard.

4. When you sense that the dynamic has changed between the two of you, start a conversation.

Note: Be sensitive to the setting, the situation, and the relationship that you have with this person. This approach carries some risk in a business situation; I recommend the aid of a trained business coach.

•• ▬▬▬ ▬

chapter 14

The Split Second

How to Handle an Irrational Person Who's Playing You Against Someone Else

MY FRIEND Mindy's six-year-old granddaughter, Joy, called her in tears. "My mom is so mean," she sobbed. "She said I couldn't eat anything at all. And I'm so hungry."

Chuckling to herself, Mindy asked to speak to this evil mom—who reported, not surprisingly, that she'd told Joy, "You can't eat any more junk food right now. Have a banana."

When Mindy got back on the line with Joy she said, "Your mommy just doesn't want you to eat too much bad food, because she cares about you. She wants you to be healthy and . . ."

Realizing that the jig was up, Joy did what most six-year-olds would do: She hung up.

In psychiatrists' terms, Joy was trying to pull a trick called *splitting*. This is a form of manipulation that involves playing one person against another.

Splitters can't take no for an answer. If they hear a negative response from the first person they talk with, they move on to the next person. In addition to bad-mouthing the first person, they delete key facts to make that person look worse. Their goal is obvious: They want the second person to side with them and say yes.

Many little kids play this game, but mature adults typically realize that it's childish. However, a surprising number of adults with low emotional IQs still try to pull this stunt. Employees try to pit two managers against each other. Aging parents attempt to split their adult children. In-laws try to split married couples. Divorced couples try to split their friends.

What makes splitters behave the way they do? In my experience, adults do it because at some point in life they experienced a big *no*— and they went from being disappointed to being depressed to being devastated about it. They're afraid of experiencing these feelings again, so they'll do anything to hear a yes.

Moira always hosted her family's Thanksgiving dinner. One year, however, her daughter-in-law wanted to do it.

Moira couldn't accept this, because she felt that if she lost control of this tradition, she'd be devastated—just like she was when her son went off to college, leaving her feeling old and useless. And she didn't ever want to feel that way again.

So first, Moira said to her daughter-in-law, "I'd prefer to have Thanksgiving at my house, like we always do."

When her daughter-in-law declined as gently and politely as possible, Moira called her son and said, "I told your wife how important this tradition is to you, but she made it very clear that your feelings didn't matter to her."

To some degree, I think splitters are a reflection of Western culture. In other cultures, people hear no a lot and learn to live with it. But we're not as accustomed to having our wishes thwarted. So instead of having a fallback position—"if Plan A doesn't work, I can try Plan B or even Plan C"—we tend to put all our eggs in one basket and say, "This has to happen."

Splitters merely take this to a higher level. A melodramatic adolescent, for example, may think, "I'll run away from home if Dad doesn't let me have a car." An employee may believe, "I'm totally screwed if I don't get this promotion." People like this turn to splitting as an act of desperation.

Also, some people gravitate toward splitting because they discovered early in life that they could play Mommy against Daddy. Since it worked so well back then, they figure it'll work now.

Splitting is a nasty little game because it can damage the relationship between the two people being split. If you think someone's trying to use you as the second party in a split—that is, trying to make you the split second—here's what to do:

1. Ask yourself, "How reasonable is the person who said no?" If there's any chance that the first person was irrational or acted like a bully, take this into consideration. If not, assume that you're dealing with a splitter.

2. Pause. Then look at the person with an innocent and puzzled expression and say, "Before I say anything, why do you think this person said no to you? What exactly did you tell her? Because we both know her pretty well, and she's generally very reasonable and isn't out to hurt you for no reason."

3. At this point, the splitter may get agitated and say something like, "You two are just alike. You always take each other's sides." If that happens, say calmly, "Okay. I'm just going to check with her and see if she has anything helpful to add about your conversation with her."

4. By now, the splitter will know that the ploy is failing and may give up. At this point, you can switch to being empathetic. Say something like, "I think the reason you're doing this is that you don't want to be disappointed, and you don't have a backup plan if you don't get your way. You want this so much, you can't think of anything else. I understand, because I've felt that way myself."

5. If you're aware of a big no that traumatized the person in the past, add, "In your mind, I think you're afraid that you'll be disappointed or devastated if this doesn't happen. I remember when you had a big disappointment before, and I know it was upsetting for you."

6. Help the person learn to become more resilient in the face of a no. Here's what I told a member of my own family recently, when he was paralyzed by the prospect of a rejection: "Nobody likes to be disappointed. But the better you can handle disappointment, the higher you can set your expectations. If a no barely causes a hiccup in your life, you can dream as big as you want. But if every no knocks you off your feet, you can only dream small."

This conversation takes patience and a little finesse. But by the end of it, you'll accomplish three goals: First, you'll establish a united front with the first person who said no. Second, you'll show the splitter that you're on to his game. Third, and most important of all, you'll help the splitter realize that no isn't the end of the world.

Usable insight ••••••••••••••••••••••••••••

Help people to accept a no and they'll feel less need to play one side against the other to get a yes.

Action Steps

1. If someone comes to you with a story about how a person you trust let him down, get the facts. If you decide that splitting is in play, call the splitter's bluff. Then talk with the splitter about handling disappointments without falling apart or slandering someone else.

2. If this is a business situation, save time for all parties by calling the person who said no into your office or contacting the person by phone while you have the splitter in your office. If possible, put the call on speakerphone. This way

you can avoid a "he said/she said" situation and quickly determine if the splitter has exaggerated something or didn't get the facts right.

• ▄▄▄

chapter 15

The Three *L*'s

Helping an Irrational Person
Cope with Extreme Fear

A PERSON trapped in intense fear is like a hamster trapped on a wheel. The person's thoughts keep spinning round and round, and as they spin, they get more and more out of control.

Here's what the soundtrack inside a fearful person's head is saying:

"The biopsy is going to show cancer. Oh my God, I'm going to die. Who will take care of my kids? I'm going to die. What am I going to do? Maybe it won't show cancer. . . . Oh my God, it's going to be cancer. And it's going to be incurable. I'm going to die. Who will take care of my kids?**"**

"Oh s#@&, I've lost one of our biggest clients. I'm going to be fired. We're going to lose the house. What will the kids do? How will I tell my wife? S#@&. What am I going to do? There aren't any other jobs out there. We're going to lose the house. . . .**"**

It's painful to watch someone you care about experiencing this kind of out-of-control fear. What's more, when you're with a fearful person who's in full amygdala hijack, it's scary for you as well. Fear is contagious, and the other person's amygdala hijack can easily spread to you. So your instinctive response is to try to talk her out of being scared.

However, you won't help matters if you try to short-circuit the person's fear response by saying, "Relax. I know things will work out just fine." That's because an intensely fearful person isn't ready to hear that message, and your words will bounce right off—or even make the person angry.

Instead, you need to accept the person's fear and then gently guide her out of it. To do this, try my three *L*'s.

The First *L*: Lean In

The first step is to realize that to a mind that's trapped in fear, the fear is reasonable. An amygdala hijack causes a person's brain to churn out a massive flood of fear-provoking chemicals including adrenaline and cortisol. These chemicals can make the person believe, "I'm going to die" or "I'm going to get fired."

So tell yourself that in this person's current reality, fear is a reasonable response. Understand that right now, this fear, while it seems out of control, is the only response that makes the person feel *in* control. That's because once the amygdala takes over, either fight, flight, or freeze sounds like a solution to what the person perceives as an assault.

The Second *L*: Look at the Reality

While a person who's fully trapped in fear isn't ready to talk about the way out, she may at least be ready to consider that a less-than-apocalyptic future is possible—if you can show the way. So at this point, your best move is to say, with great empathy, "Let's find out what's really going on here."

Then talk about the situation, exploring all possible scenarios and outcomes. Remember, you're not saying, "It'll be fine." You're simply introducing the idea that it might turn out fine.

As you talk, focus on three questions:

▸ Is the terrible thing the person anticipates really the most likely outcome of the situation?

▸ Is it just as likely, or even more likely, that things will work out okay?

▸ Has the person or someone the person knows survived similar crises in the past? If so, is it likely that this crisis is manageable, too?

For example, you can say things such as:

▸ "Your biopsy could come back positive, and if it does, we'll handle it, just like we handled it when I was sick. But I remember the doctor saying that it's much more likely to be negative. And she also said that even if it's positive, this type of cancer is highly treatable. "

▸ "I guess there's a chance that Dave may fire you. But there's also a good chance that given your track record, he'll just get mad and then get over it. The world didn't come to an end when I lost that big account last year. Remember?"

As you explore various possibilities, the person will gradually recover from the amygdala hijack and begin to think rationally. Once you sense that the person is beginning to let go of the fear, it's time for your next move.

The Third *L*: Lead the Person into the Future

Now that the person is ready to start thinking a little more clearly, say something like, "Given the current reality, what is a realistic action to take now?"

Creating a plan of action together at this point will help the person get past being stuck in fear. So say something like:

▶ "Is there anything we can do right now to ease your stress while you're waiting for your test results? Why don't we watch a movie or go for a run?"

▶ "Is there a way you can regain the account? If not, are there other accounts you can go after? Or do you think you can expand the work you're doing for your existing accounts?"

One technique I use to help people get unstuck from fear and move forward is something I call *solving for simultaneous experiences*. You know how in algebra class you solved for simultaneous equations? If you knew what x and y were, then you could solve for z. Similarly, when people get stuck in a thought, a feeling, or an action, one good approach is to move them forward by focusing on one or both of the other two variables.

For example, if people are stuck in a thought like, "My life is ruined," unstick them by taking them shopping, which gets them to act, or put on a fun movie that will get them to feel. Or if they're in the office and are stuck in an action (such as checking their email constantly to see if they're being summoned to a meeting with the human resources director), get them to think by asking for their advice about a project, or get them to feel by talking with them about their kids.

As you guide a fearful person through the three *L*'s, remember: Be gentle, be empathetic, and above all, be patient. It will take time for the person's amygdala to cool down from a boil to a simmer, and for her levels of fear chemicals to dissipate. But it'll happen.

One evening a few months ago, I called a colleague, Katy, to talk about a project we were working on together. The project was running late, but I was sure we'd get it done on time. And even if we didn't, I figured that we could get an extension.

Katy, however, had descended into a total panic about the project, and (lucky me) I'd called her right in the middle of her meltdown.

"There's no way we can get this done on time," she said hysterically. "And we'll be legally liable. And my business will be ruined. And . . ."

For a few seconds, I could feel myself slipping into an amygdala hijack as well. After all, it was a big project. And if Katy melted down, I'd have trouble finishing it alone.

Luckily, I'm good at putting my shrink hat on. Recognizing my own imminent amygdala hijack, I told myself, "Stop it." Then, setting my own feelings aside, I looked at the situation from Katy's point of view. She is, as she cheerfully admits, "the world's most pessimistic pessimist." She'd also lost a couple of days on the project due to an illness. The project was, indeed, a very challenging one. And she'd worked on it from 4 a.m. to 8 p.m. that day, without even stopping to eat. You can understand that in her tired, hungry, naturally pessimistic state of mind, feeling fearful was a totally reasonable response.

To help her work through her fear, I let Katy vent. And vent. And vent. And then, when she started winding down, we talked about where we really stood. In reality, we were working with a nice company that wasn't going to sue us if we wound up finishing the job a week late. And while the project was a tough one, we were making good progress despite some major roadblocks.

Eventually, when Katy was more or less ready to consider the possibility that the world wasn't coming to an end, we talked about what to do next. I said I'd call the company and ensure that our deadline was flexible. She came up with a few possible solutions for our roadblocks. And by the time we hung up, she was a big step closer to sane.

Oh, and the project? It turned out fine. As I mentioned in Chapter 7, breakdowns often lead to breakthroughs, and by the day after our talk, Katy had everything back on track.

When you use the three *L*'s with fearful people, be aware that in addition to venting their fear, they may sometimes lash out at you in what I call fearful aggression. (This is the same reason why timid dogs tend to bite people.) When you recognize that this lashing out is part of a fearful person's M.O., you'll be better able to accept it and handle it calmly. Simply let the person vent, and then return to your game plan.

Finally, if you're dealing with a person who frequently has fear freak-outs, introduce that person to the "Oh F#@& to OK" speed drill I outlined in Chapter 7. This drill can stop an amygdala hijack in its tracks—and an ounce of prevention is better than a ton of *L*'s.

Usable insight •

If you can lean into someone's fear, you can prevent the person from panicking.

Action Steps
When a person is exhibiting an extreme fear reaction, remember these three rules:

1. **Lean in.** Recognize that the person's response is reasonable from her viewpoint.

2. **Look at the reality.** Help the person see the situation in a more rational way.

3. **Lead the person to a solution.** Together, come up with a realistic action plan for moving forward.

chapter 16

The Butter-Up

Getting a Know-It-All
to Behave

FEW PEOPLE annoy us more than know-it-alls. I'm not talking here about subject-matter experts who aren't arrogant but simply love to share what they know. I'm talking about the know-it-alls who offend you by rubbing their supposed superiority in your face.

But are these people's actions crazy? Yes—because they constantly sabotage themselves, and the know-it-alls who really are smart are wasting their own potential. Chet, for example, was a master at stepping on his own feet by insisting on getting his own way.

When it came to marketing his firm's IT services, Chet was brilliant. He understood the technology, and he understood his customers' needs. Under his direction, his firm's marketing department initially posted win after win.

But over time, the people who worked under Chet lost their enthusiasm for his leadership. Eventually, they even began to undermine him as their passive-aggressive "F#@& you" for the way he treated them. And when I talked with them, I could see why.

In meeting after meeting, Chet expected people to accept his ideas unconditionally while he openly mocked or belittled theirs.

He said things like, "Yeah, your idea would work great—if we were back in the 1980s." He rolled his eyes when people politely questioned his own ideas. And he often cut them off with a curt comment like, "You're wrong," or, "That's stupid," or even worse, "You're stupid."

As a result, the team developed an intense dislike for Chet. In fact, when I met them, I could see the gleam in their eyes as they anticipated him getting his just deserts. They couldn't wait for me to deliver a massive smackdown.

But I didn't.

Instead, I told Chet what an important asset he was to his company.

"What?" you say. Read on.

Why do know-it-alls like Chet act the way they do? Because early in life they learn that being snide or sarcastic gets them what they want (in the short term). By offending others, they push their victims back on their heels, and by the time those victims bounce back, the know-it-alls are off to their next targets.

However, know-it-alls aren't completely oblivious to the long-term effects of their actions. On some level, they sense that people don't like them. That's because deep down, they know they wouldn't like people who talked down to them.

Unfortunately, because they're irrational, know-it-alls don't act on this information in a smart way. They don't say, "People think I'm a jerk, and I need to change my behavior." Instead, they say, "People dislike me because they're stupid and incompetent."

This convinces the know-it-alls that they need to double down on quashing the spirits of their victims. It was probably the actions of a know-it-all that gave rise to the expression "add insult to injury," because that's exactly what these people do.

What's the best way to handle know-it-alls? Most people react by becoming defensive or sullen. But that just makes know-it-alls nastier by reinforcing their idea that people are stupid, causing them to feel even more contemptuous.

Therefore, no matter how crazy it sounds, you'll want to do just the opposite. Your best strategy is to lean fully into these people's reality—which is that as geniuses, they're entitled to more respect than they get.

When I first met Chet, I knew he didn't want to be in the room with me. His body language—cold eyes, crossed arms—clearly said, "This guy is a jerk. Just another moron. I'm so smart and bring so much to this company, I shouldn't have to put up with this."

I'm used to facing people like Chet. His attitude didn't faze me. Instead, I looked at him with a small smile and said, "Do you know how incredibly smart you are?"

My question caught Chet completely off guard, and he looked a little taken aback. "What?" he asked.

"No, I mean it," I said. "You are really smart at what you do. In fact, from what I've heard, you're gifted. Brilliant, even." I cited examples I'd heard: marketing innovations he'd spearheaded, clients he'd scored, costs he'd cut.

As I talked, Chet's bewilderment disarmed him. No sarcasm, no condescension. Just bewilderment. And then I said, "That's the good news. Now for the bad news: When you're as bright as you are, you have a responsibility not to distract people from your amazing gift. But that's what you do. Just when people are on the verge of buying into what you're saying, you hit them with sarcasm or condescension and they 'buy out.' You're leaving results on the table that your brilliance deserves, and that's foolish. This is dishonoring your God-given gift. And it means that God should have given it to someone else. In order to deserve a gift like this, you need to use it wisely."

Next, to add the icing to the cake, I said, "If you turned the people who want to kill you into people who would want to kill *for* you, the kind of results you could get would absolutely blow your mind—not to mention advance your career and turbocharge the company's future."

How's that for smooth? I'd slathered so much butter on my
message that it was easy for Chet to swallow it whole. And he did.

In general, the game that know-it-alls like to play is tag. Only
their version is: I can tag you (by demeaning or belittling you) but
you can't tag me (because my confidence in my own brilliance is
unshakable). And you can't win at this game, so don't play it.

Instead, try doing something the know-it-all won't expect: Agree
that this person is incredibly smart. Flatter him for being so bright.
Use words like *wise*, *insightful*, *intelligent*, *genius*, *brilliant*. And then,
deliver your message: "People would really appreciate your brilliance if you didn't incite them to want to sabotage you." When you
do this, your words will be in complete alignment with the person's
high self-image, and that will make your medicine easier to accept.

Now, if you're thoroughly fed up with a know-it-all, it may set
your teeth on edge to deliver this kind of flattery. But the key here
is to keep your mind on your ultimate goal: getting the person to
behave better. And if flattery is what it takes, it's more than worth a
cringe or two.

TIP

There are some true geniuses who bully their entire organizations.
Flattery won't work with these people because they're narcissists
(which I discussed in Chapter 4). So don't try this approach with
someone who has an extremely high IQ but lacks the social and emotional intelligence to act appropriately in normal business situations.

Usable insight •

The more you butter up the egos of know-it-alls, the less
likely they are to talk down to you.

Action Steps

1. If you're dealing with a know-it-all, identify the areas in
which the person truly is smart.

2. When you meet with the person, lead with this type of information. For instance, say things like:

- ▶ "Your talent is amazing."
- ▶ "You're the best designer we have on staff."
- ▶ "Your ideas are fresh and new."
- ▶ "You have an outstanding eye for color."
- ▶ "Your latest presentation was fascinating."

3. Next, describe how the know-it-all's actions are self-defeating, but do it in a way that reinforces your flattery. For example, say, "Our younger designers have so much to learn from you. Unfortunately, when you're sarcastic or cut them down, they tune out—and that means they're not getting the benefit of your expertise. I think if you can find a way to approach them as a mentor rather than as a critic, they'll learn far more from you."

● ▬▬▬

chapter 17

Executive
Order

Getting a Martyr
to Accept Help

DO YOU KNOW people who simply refuse to ask for help, no matter how overwhelmed they become? This is an interesting kind of crazy that masquerades as selflessness but actually stems from an intense fear of hearing the word *no*.

These people think of themselves as self-sacrificing and even noble. (A classic example is the martyr mom, who insists on doing all the chores and waiting on her family hand and foot while expecting nothing in return.) In reality, however, they can't ask for help because unconsciously they know that getting a no in response will infuriate them—especially if they feel entitled to a yes. That's because (much like those splitters I talked about in Chapter 14) they've experienced some devastating nos in the past. And they unconsciously believe that a similar event now will send them spiraling back into the intense anger those past rejections caused.

If you manage people like this in your job, their refusal to ask for help when they're in over their heads can prevent you from reaching your targets. (That's because they usually won't let on that they're overwhelmed until it's too late to meet their goals.) Often, they'll leave you frustrated or even furious because they'll put your job in jeopardy. And if you live with someone like this, you'll become irritated by the constant martyr act and the guilt it provokes in you.

What's the solution? Don't ask a martyr if she needs help. Instead, order her to accept it.

Dana was a project editor for an online education provider. Her boss, Joel, gave his team plenty of freedom and trusted them to let him know if they were struggling.

But Dana didn't let him know. Instead, she took on every project he asked her to do, and if he asked, "Do you need Matt or Bonnie to help with this?" she always said no. So Joel assumed that everything was fine.

Dana was good at her job, and for a while she managed to carry a heavy workload without any help (although it meant putting in extra hours on weekends and nights without Joel's knowledge). Even when things started slipping, she glossed over the situation in her weekly reports. But it all came to a head when Joel found out that two of their most crucial online medical transcription courses wouldn't be done by deadline. He was furious with Dana—and his boss was furious with him.

Worried about his own position, Joel consulted with me. He told me he wanted to keep Dana on his team because she was an outstanding editor, but he wasn't willing to jeopardize his own career for her.

My guess, based on my experience with many situations like this in the past, was that Dana wasn't just being stubborn——that she couldn't ask for help. So I offered him a work-around.

A week later, Joel scheduled a meeting with Dana. At this meeting, he said, "I'm really impressed by your talent, and by your willingness to tackle big projects. But I've noticed that you have trouble asking for help, even when you're struggling."

He continued in an empathetic tone, "I'm guessing that in the past, people have let you down when you asked for help. And I think right now, your productivity is dying for the sins of those in your past who disappointed you when you needed help—or even made you feel guilty for asking, so you never wanted to ask again. Does that make sense?"

Dana replied, "Oh my God. It's like you've met my parents."

Joel laughed. "Well, here's how both of us are going to fix this situation," he said. "As of this moment, I'm giving you a direct order: When you're overwhelmed, you are to ask for help. This is not a suggestion. As I said, it's an order. That's because when you don't ask for help, you're not just hurting our department, you're hurting yourself. And I don't want that to happen, because you're a great person and a great team member."

Then Joel walked Dana through each of the projects on her list. "Tell me what help you need here," he said. And he refused to take no for an answer.

As Joel learned, the best way to deal with a person who can't ask for help is to take the decision out of the person's hands. This completely changes the dynamic, transforming it from asking for help to following an order.

Two important points about this approach:

▸ Make sure that people follow through on the person's requests for help. If they don't, it'll just amplify her fear of rejection.

▸ Once a month or so, check in with the person and say, "Give me some examples of where you've asked for help." This will give her additional motivation to follow your order.

Now, if you're the boss of the person in question, this trick is pretty easy to pull off because you're already in charge. It's a little trickier if you're dealing with a spouse or significant other. In that case, you're equal partners, and issuing orders might get your partner's back up. So you'll need to phrase your "demand" carefully. Here's an example:

❝ It's amazing how you juggle your job and the house and the kids. If I don't say that often enough, I apologize. But there's something else I'd like to say: I'm worried about you. You do a lot, and you can't ask for help. And I think it's because you've asked for help in the past and you didn't get it—or people even made you feel ashamed for asking.

But I want you to know that I'm not those people. I love you; I respect you; I know how hard you work, and I will never intentionally let you down if you ask me for help.

Now I'm going to do something I've never, ever done in our relationship and probably will never do again—I'm going to give you an order: When you're exhausted because you have too much to do, ask me for help.

To show how important this is to me, I'm going to check every week to see if there's something you could have and should have asked me for help with but didn't.**"**

Initially, your partner might not know how to respond to this (or may repeat, "I really don't need help"). But be firm, just like Joel was, and don't take no for an answer. Afterward, whenever you see your partner taking on too much work, say, "Give me two things on your to-do list right now."

Then smile and say, "That's an order."

Usable insight ●

Show me a person who can't say, "I need help," and I'll show you a person who can't tolerate hearing *no*.

Action Steps

1. Identify the people in your life who can't ask for help.

2. Wait for a time when these people are in a receptive mood.

3. Then order them—don't ask them—to ask for help.

● ●

chapter 18

Coup
Contrecoup

Turning an Irrational
Person's M.O. to
Your Own Advantage

IF YOU FALL in the shower and hit your head, your brain will suffer an injury at the spot where you hit it. In addition, it'll suffer an injury on the opposite side, as your brain bounces off one side of your skull and caroms into the other side. In medicine, we call this type of injury *coup contrecoup*.

What does that have to do with crazy? In the types of situations I'll talk about in this chapter, irrational people will attempt to injure you by being nasty or sarcastic. But you're going to take their crazy and shove it right back in the opposite direction. Coup contrecoup.

As you can guess, this is a risky thing to do. However, there are smart ways and not-so-smart ways to do it, and I'm going to minimize your risk by showing you the smart way.

First, however, let me illustrate the not-so-smart way.

By the time I finished medical school and started my internship, I knew I wasn't cut out to treat cancer, deliver babies, or perform hernia operations. Instead, I was fascinated by the mind, and I was discovering that I had a real knack for getting through to unhappy, angry, or even psychotic people.

Nonetheless, I gave it my all as I rotated through the different medical specialties. And most of the doctors I worked with respected my hard work. But one of them didn't.

This doctor—let's call him Dr. Jerk—was a surgical fellow. He was very good at what he did, but his M.O. was to make people feel small and stupid. As a result of his nasty manner, his students learned far less from him than they should have (because they were terrified of being mocked if they asked the wrong questions), and most of the staff despised him.

As an arrogant surgeon, Dr. Jerk was especially scornful of psychiatrists. And needless to say, he never missed an opportunity to let me know it.

One day, I was following along as Dr. Jerk made rounds with a surgical resident and several medical students. At each bedside, he'd ask us a few questions. I was doing a fine job of answering, but that didn't stop him from going on the attack.

At one point, he turned to me and asked a question. But before I even had two seconds to formulate my answer, he looked at me and said, "I don't know why I bother even asking *you.*"

Up to then, I'd tolerated Dr. Jerk's sarcasm over and over again. But that day, I'd had enough. So I decided to throw his own M.O. right back at him.

For a moment, I simply stood there silently and stared at him. "What are you looking at?" he asked me.

I smiled slightly. "I'm just thinking that your tone toward me will be very different in 20 years when you bring your kid to me because you f#@&ed him up."

His eyes widened for a split second, as if I'd struck him. And then, turning on his heel, he marched us off to the next patient's bed.

Luckily, I got away with my insolence that day. Moreover, I like to think that Dr. Jerk was a tiny bit humbler after our encounter. Somewhere down the line, another budding psychiatrist may have avoided getting his soul crushed thanks to my big mouth.

However, my approach was clearly risky. And it definitely wasn't too smart. So here's a better way to pull off a coup contrecoup.

First, recognize that the person you're dealing with uses sarcasm as a weapon—and as a defense. This person feels in control only when you're too cowed to ask questions or make assertions that might be threatening. For instance, Dr. Jerk rarely had to worry about an intern or medical student saying, "What about the new procedure outlined in this month's *Annals of Surgery?*" (which Dr. Jerk hadn't read). We might think it, but we wouldn't say it. His actions were crazy—because they lost him the respect of his colleagues and poisoned his relationships with us—but they worked in the short term by keeping us from poking any holes in his ego balloon.

Similarly, the sarcastic people in your own life want to make you feel smaller, less important, and less competent. Many of these people will be know-it-alls. Others, however, will use sarcasm to hide their own insecurity. (Think teenagers.)

No matter what their underlying agenda is, people like this want you to feel insecure about your own abilities and opinions so you won't question theirs. Once you understand this dynamic, you'll be able to keep your own emotional response under control.

To prepare for an encounter with a sarcastic person, anticipate his sarcasm. When you do this, you'll be ready for it. In fact, it may even make you smile and think, "I called it."

Then, when you speak with the person, watch for your coup contrecoup moment. This is where you'll turn the tables on him by saying, "Gotcha"—but politely.

Here's an example:

You: Here's our idea. We've looked at the feedback from our customers, and they say they'd like the software better if we made it more user-friendly. So we're wondering if your team can . . .

Mitch: (Makes an impatient noise.)

You: . . . redesign the interface so it's easier for customers to . . .

Mitch: (Snorting derisively) I see. You're not just the customer service manager, you're the interface expert. (Snorting again.) I don't know why I'm wasting my time with you when you know nothing about technology.

You: (After pausing a moment, smiling to yourself, and saying "Gotcha"—and then pausing some more to throw him off balance) I don't know either.

Mitch: What?

You: Well, I don't want to waste any more of your time, and I saw that whatever I said, you'd disagree with me. So I thought it made sense to cut to the chase.

What did you do here? You anticipated where Mitch's crazy would ultimately take him, and then you went there first. In essence, you hit him right in the face with his own M.O.

When you go straight for the knockout, you immediately stop the person from escalating his attack. That's because the only way for this person to be right is to make you wrong. And that means that he has to not act nasty or sarcastic from that point on.

How cool is that?

This approach works with kids as well as adults. In fact, it's a natural with teenagers. For instance, imagine that you're trying to ensure that a hormonal teen finishes an important project on time. Here's how your coup contrecoup might go:

You: How are you doing on that term paper?

Teen: I'm working on it. Just like the last time you asked me five seconds ago.

You: (Pausing first, while keeping your expression open and curious) I get it.

Teen: What?

You: (In a calm, empathetic tone of voice, with a touch of humor) Right now, you want me to get off your damned back and leave you alone. Is that right?

Teen: What?

You: I was just thinking about what was going on, and rather than getting my blood pressure up, I thought I'd just say out loud what I'm guessing you're thinking. And I'm guessing that's, "Get off my damned back and leave me alone."

Teen: That's not what I was going to say. I'm just frustrated. I'm sick of this stupid paper, and I don't know what to write, and I'm not going to get it done on time. . . .

At this stage, your teen will still be irrational but will start to lean into your sanity. By using conversation extenders ("Tell me more about that"), you can help your child to vent his frustration and get to a calmer state. And maybe the term paper will actually get done.

One of the most important elements of this strategy is the pause. It takes practice to get this pause exactly right. Not too long, and not too short, the pause is the cornerstone of your coup contrecoup because it accomplishes three things:

▸ It allows you to center yourself.

▸ It signals to the irrational person that trying to provoke you won't work.

▸ It says, "I'm on to you," forcing the irrational person to abandon sarcasm and try another approach.

Also, strive for an attitude of relaxed, calm empathy. In fact, be a little playful. For instance, when you tell your teen, "Right now, you want me to get off your damned back and leave you alone," let a little smile play on your lips. Any hint of anger or defensiveness will lead the irrational person to push back, while a spoonful of sugar— in the form of empathy and humor—will make your medicine go down more easily.

Finally, realize that your conversation isn't over after your coup contrecoup. Instead, it's just beginning. But this time around, if you're lucky, it'll be a meeting of the minds—not a major headache.

Usable insight •

Sarcasm is disguised aggression, and sometimes, it's fine to punch back.

Action Steps

1. Before you talk with a sarcastic person, preview your conversation mentally. What verbal barbs is the person likely to throw at you? What emotions will he attempt to provoke in you? What state of mind are you in right now? Are you ready for action?

2. Now, mentally cut to the chase by thinking of what the person will do or say in order to end your conversation. Does he usually cut off communication by saying something like, "That's a dumb idea," or, "Get out of my life," or, "That's above your pay grade"?

3. When you talk to the person, wait for the first or second nasty or sarcastic remark. At that point, pause. Keep your expression calm and even smile a little.

4. Then turn the person's barb into your coup contrecoup by calmly tossing it right back in the opposite direction. For instance, say, "This is where you say that this is above my pay grade," or, "I can see where this is going, and this is where you're going to ask me to get out of your life."

5. When the person denies this (even though it's true), he will need a little time to regroup and come up with a new (and generally much better) M.O. Be patient and allow him to vent during this stage. Then steer the conversation in a better direction.

• ▬▬▬▬

chapter 19

The Kiss-Off (and the Gentle Kiss-Off)

Saying No to a Manipulator

MANIPULATORS are a special kind of crazy. Their behavior doesn't work in the long run, because it drives most of their allies away. But it works exceptionally well in the short run, and that's as far as these people can see.

Manipulators want to turn their problems into your problems, and they'll succeed if you let them. These people will leave you emotionally drained, and sometimes financially drained as well. And no matter how much you help them, they'll be back the next week—or even the next day—wanting you to fix their latest problem.

In *Just Listen*, I offered one tip for getting rid of many manipulators. That's simply to wait until they ask you to do something and say, "I'd be glad to. And in return, here's what you can do for me." This works almost every time with minor-league manipulators, but it's often insufficient when you're dealing with pros. In the latter case, you'll probably need something stronger.

I know of two good ways to approach these extreme manipulators. I call them the Kiss-Off and the Gentle Kiss-Off. If you're a gentle soul, go for the second one. But if you're gutsy and you're not scared of confrontations, by all means try the first one.

The Kiss-Off

Picture a needy and manipulative person; let's call him John. He's accosted you every day for a week, whining or even fully melting down and asking or demanding that you help solve his problems.

The next time John starts in on you:

1. Let him vent, blame, whine, or complain.

2. Pause.

3. Reply: "You know, it'll either (A) get better, (B) get worse, (C) stay the same, or (D) none of the above."

4. Let him vent and rant some more. (And he will, because he'll be upset that his manipulation didn't work this time.)

5. Pause.

6. Say: "Oops. Excuse me. I guess the answer must be 'E.' And I don't know what that is."

7. Let him vent and rant even more.

8. Pause.

9. Reply: "Well, it looks like I'm not going to be of much assistance. Hope it turns out okay. Sorry, but I gotta go now."

10. If John needs to have the last word, let him have it. Then say good-bye and get up and leave (or hang up if you're on the phone).

In many cases, people like John will come back within 24 hours to apologize. That's because you remained calm instead of becoming defensive or retaliating, which increased the contrast between your sane behavior and his craziness. If you don't hear from him right away, wait until he contacts you, because the next communication needs to come from him. If you give in first, it means he's succeeded. So sit tight and wait. In the end, you'll win.

Here's a variant of the in-your-face Kiss-Off that I like to use. In this version, as in the last one, you let the person vent. When she is finished, you calmly say, "Okay, I understand. Now what?" Then, after the person keeps venting, you say, "That seems like a lot for you to have to fix, so I'd suggest you get started sooner rather than later. What's your first step?" If she continues to vent, say, "I think I'll be going, and I'll check back with you later to see what you decided to do." Then get up calmly and leave.

The Gentle Kiss-Off

If you're a sensitive person, there's a good chance that you just read my instructions for tackling manipulators head-on and said, "Oh, no—there's no way I can do that."

That's okay, because there's another way to take on manipulators. It's gentle. It's kind. And most of the time, it works.

All you need to do is say, "Stop."

Joan and Nancy used to work together at a TV network in Chicago. Three years ago, Joan retired.

But Nancy couldn't live without her. She called Joan constantly with questions and complaints. How should I handle this project? What happens if I miss this deadline? They won't give me a promotion. My new boss is terrible.

Then things escalated. Last year, the network asked Nancy to attend a meeting in Dubai. But without Joan to lean on, Nancy was a basket case. She had two fainting spells and went to see a physician, who told her she was having panic attacks and hyperventilating. Nancy told her boss that she couldn't go to Dubai because she might have another attack.

After her fainting spells, Nancy started calling Joan even more often, exhausting her friend. Finally, Joan turned to me for advice. While she knew that Nancy's behavior was irrational, she didn't know what to do about it.

But I had a pretty good idea.

I asked Joan, "Do you think of yourself as one of Nancy's close friends?"

"I'm her best friend. But she's really getting to me," she replied.

"Okay. I'm assuming that as her best friend, you want to help her. And the last thing you want to do is make her worse. Is that true?" I asked.

"Of course," Joan answered.

"Does listening to her help her?" I asked.

Joan hesitated. "For a little while."

"But then she calls you a day later about another crisis that she wants you to solve. So is she getting any better at handling things?"

"I guess not," she admitted.

"So you're a good friend and you have good intentions," I said. "But Nancy isn't getting better. In fact, she's getting even more needy and manipulative. And I'm guessing that she's already burned out her other friends."

Joan laughed wryly. "Yeah. That's another one of the things she complains to me about."

Now, I don't particularly like the term *enabler*. But that's what Joan was, and she needed to break that pattern.

"So while you want to help Nancy," I said, "you're actually enabling her to keep acting helpless. And she's making you crazy as a result. Is that true?"

"Yes—I guess so," Joan said tentatively.

"Which one?" I asked. "Yes, or you guess so?"

"Okay . . . yes, for God's sake," she said, finally venting her frustration.

"Then here's what I suggest," I said. "The next time Nancy starts to vent, let her go for five seconds. Then, firmly but kindly, say, 'I need to stop you for a moment.' Don't cut her off immediately. But picture her as a 747 taking off, with you standing in its path.

You want to stop her before she picks up enough speed to run you down. When you do, she'll probably say something like, 'Huh?' or 'What?' But don't let her start again."

Joan nodded. "Then what do I do?"

I told Joan to tell Nancy: "I need to stop you because I'm doing something wrong as your friend. I see that when you vent to me, you feel better, but then you're not motivated to deal with your problems. In essence, I'm enabling you to stay stuck in bad situations. And as your friend, I can't and won't continue to do that. So going forward, I'm going to interrupt this kind of conversation just like I did today. Then I'm going to say that I get that you're scared or upset. So what's the first thing you should do to deal with this situation?"

Take a closer look at what I asked Joan to do here. I didn't tell her to say something like, "You expect me to solve all your problems," or, "I'm not your mother!" That's because fighting back at crazy rather than leaning into it won't work. And I didn't tell her to try the more blunt Kiss-Off approach, because for people like Joan, who are terrified of confrontation, this approach is too traumatic.

Instead, she's going to disarm Nancy by saying, in effect, "This is my fault"—which, to a large degree, is true. Then she's going to introduce a new dynamic: "Yes, you have a problem. Tell me what you're going to do about it."

This approach isn't always effective, and it may only work in the short run if you're dealing with someone who has a serious issue like borderline personality disorder. But it does work a lot.

So take your pick: the in-your-face Kiss-Off or the kinder Gentle Kiss-Off. Either one is better than spending your life playing savior to people who need to save themselves.

Usable insight •

If a person wants you to say yes but needs you to say no, say no.

Action Steps

1. Identify the people in your life who shove all of their problems off on you.

2. Recognize that you aren't helping them by allowing them to manipulate you.

3. Recognize that you aren't helping yourself by letting them impose on you.

4. Starting with the most demanding people first, use the Kiss-Off or the Gentle Kiss-Off to teach these people to shoulder their own burdens.

• ▬▬▬▬▬

chapter 20

Frenemies

Handling a "Toxic
Deflector" at Work

FEW THINGS cost CEOs and managers the respect of their employees more than being played by the people I call toxic deflectors. You know exactly who I'm talking about. It's the people who do things such as:

▶ Manage up superbly.

▶ Cozy up to the boss by providing intelligence on the q.t.

▶ Court the favor of the boss by performing personal favors that are often more in the boss's personal interest than the company's best interest.

▶ Throw highly competent colleagues (who might threaten their position) under the bus by bad-mouthing them.

▶ Manipulate bosses who have little skill in reading other people.

▶ Exhibit much more skill in playing politics than in carrying out their responsibilities.

▶ Appear much smarter to the people above them than to their peers or the people below them.

▶ Care primarily about the security of their own position and not about the needs of anyone else, including the boss they're currying favor with.

▶ Deflect any blame or criticism for their actions or failure to act.

▶ Feel threatened by high achievers, fearing that their own incompetence will be exposed.

▶ Keep anyone off the scent of their inadequacies and devious behavior by blaming others, making excuses, or minimizing others' criticisms.

▶ Stop at nothing to prevent being found out.

Toxic deflectors are the people who give politics a bad name. Playing politics is often necessary when you need to get an important job done. But being political is about doing whatever is required to further your own interests. That's the toxic deflector's agenda.

The biggest key to understanding toxic deflectors is that they're incompetent—and deep down they know it. There's a saying that people who aren't able to take advantage of opportunity—by being first movers, innovators, or superspecialists—take advantage of people instead. That's a toxic deflector's M.O.

This is crazy behavior because in the long run, toxic deflectors wind up making enemies of nearly everyone. Peers and subordinates quickly learn to despise these people and offer them as little support as possible. And higher-ups eventually dump them when they discover that they're wreaking havoc on departments or entire companies. But until that happens, toxic deflectors can make life miserable for the people who have to work with them.

Sitting across from me, Carmen said bluntly, "I can't stand Gail." Carmen, the assistant public relations director for a manufacturer in the Midwest, told me she'd loved her job at first. But working under Gail was taking a huge toll.

"She just fakes doing her job," Carmen said. "She comes in around 10, leaves around 2 for a late lunch, and never comes back."

Luckily for Gail, Carmen always picked up the slack. But Gail made sure she didn't get credit for it.

"Take a look at our monthly reports," Carmen said. "When Gail actually does something, she writes, 'I made all of the arrangements for our highly successful conference.' But when I do something, she writes, 'Our department completed this major project.' My name never even shows up. In fact, the only time she mentions me is when a project isn't a total success. Then she tries to pin it on me."

Later that day, I talked with one of Gail's fellow managers. Sandy, the head of material control, also viewed Gail as a slacker. And Sandy offered up another interesting insight. "Gail plays our CEO," she told me. "While the men might not recognize what she's up to, the women all do."

Gerald, the company's CEO, was a short, pudgy, 60ish man who vainly attempted to hide his balding head with a comb-over. When I'd met with him, he hadn't struck me as the brightest bulb. And according to Sandy, Gail—an attractive blonde in her mid-30s— took advantage of this in more ways than one.

"First," Sandy told me, "she inflates her own accomplishments, because she knows that Gerald doesn't really know what she's doing. Second, she ingratiates herself with him by inflating his accomplishments. And finally, she does what we women call her 'slut act.'"

Sandy told me about Gail's mannerisms around Gerald—the way she occasionally touched his arm when she made a point and the flashes of cleavage she showed when she leaned over to hand him a paper. "We all laugh about it behind her back," Sandy said. "But we also resent it, because we're working our butts off and she's getting away with murder."

How is it that toxic deflectors get into organizations undetected? Actually, they don't get into all organizations—just the vulnerable ones. And often, what makes a company vulnerable is a flawed (but not necessarily toxic) leader who can be charmed and manipulated by such people.

These leaders themselves are often covering up some serious shortcomings that they fear will be exposed. Many have a fair amount of charm and charisma, but they often come up short in business acumen. By giving them cover (and stroking their egos), toxic deflectors make these bosses feel more competent and admirable than they are.

What can you do if you're a high achiever who's a threat to a toxic deflector who uses her manipulative skills to discredit you? Sadly, if this manipulator bedazzles your boss, there's not much you can do to change the boss's opinion. You have as much chance of turning the situation around as you do of talking sense into a parent who's in total denial about an oh-so-charming child's lying and stealing.

There is, however, one approach you may want to consider. It's based on the fact that the toxic deflector has two primary goals: to curry favor with the boss and to keep from having her own incompetence revealed. The approach is to help the toxic deflector achieve both of these goals. But it comes with a caution: Don't try it until you've given it a lot of thought and played out how it could backfire and make things even worse. In particular, think carefully about how this may affect your relationships with your other colleagues.

Realistically, you will never make this person your friend or ally, because you will always be more competent than her. You will always be a threat. But if you demonstrate that you can also forward the person's agenda, you will at least move from enemy to frenemy. And that will make the person far less of a threat to you.

Here's how to do it:

1. Think of a true, remarkable, and special competency that the toxic deflector possesses. Virtually everyone, even the most incompetent person, has some talent or ability.

2. Think of a way this unique competency could significantly help your company.

3. Brainstorm with the toxic deflector about this special opportunity.

4. Help the toxic deflector come up with a plan and carry it through successfully.

5. Find a way to bring the result to your boss's attention, causing the boss to praise the toxic deflector.

Be aware that the toxic deflector might smell a rat and wonder why in the world you're trying to be helpful when she's always striving to undermine you. If she calls you on this, be prepared with an answer. The simplest response is, "I want to support your priorities so that we can all win together." A more honest one is, "I was getting tired of us always being at odds with each other and tired of my resenting you for it. So I decided to take a step back and objectively think about some of your special skills and how you might use them to help the company and advance your own position here."

If the person stares at you, still dumbfounded that you actually care about her needs, you can add, "I know a lot of grudge holders, and they're miserable to be around—and miserable themselves. I decided to do something to make sure I don't turn into one."

And guess what?

From your perspective, that's probably the truth.

Usable insight ●

Keep your friends close, and your toxic deflectors closer.

Action Steps

1. If there's a toxic deflector in your life, observe the person carefully and identify her strengths, even if they lie outside of her job description.

2. Think of a way to put these strengths to use in your company or organization.

3. Get the toxic deflector on board with your plan, and help her succeed in carrying it out.

4. Spread the word of this success—and in particular, make sure the toxic deflector's higher-ups hear about it.

● ███

chapter 21

I Know What You're Hiding

Getting a Sociopath
out of Your Life

THIS CHAPTER is about sociopaths. Technically, they don't belong in this book at all, which is why I've shoehorned them in at the end of this section.

Sociopathic people are ruthless, self-centered, shallow, manipulative, and completely lacking in compassion. In short, they're evil. But successful sociopaths aren't irrational. They're actually cold-bloodedly sane, and sadly for the rest of us, they sometimes turn out to be successful as CEOs and politicians (at least in the short term).

However, many sociopaths continue to escalate their behavior because they feel increasingly invulnerable. And that's when they become both irrational and very dangerous.

If you encounter sociopaths in your own life, the best way to deal with them is *not* to deal with them. If you're tangled up with someone who's a sociopath and it's possible to escape, do whatever it takes to get out of the relationship, even if it means taking a financial hit. And do it now rather than later, because sociopaths will dig their claws in deeper over time.

Often, however, it's not so easy to free yourself from a sociopath. If you're in this situation, there's one powerful technique that may enable you to break the person's hold over you. I call it I Know

What You're Hiding, and it's one time when you won't try to convince someone that you're an ally. Instead, you'll show the person that you're a threat.

Here's how a friend of mine used this approach successfully.

"Doc, do you know how to deal with a sociopath?" Jerry, an investment adviser and a friend of mine, asked me.

"What exactly do you mean?" I asked.

"I think my assistant might be one," he said. "A year and a half ago my office was destroyed by a mud slide after a torrential rain. I felt very vulnerable. At that time, I'd become acquainted with a guy named Glenn. I felt really sorry for him because he told me he'd had lymphoma and that he'd been forced to file for bankruptcy.

"One day, Glenn asked if he could do some work for me. He said he could help me find a new office and also arrange for some public seminars to help me publicize my work. Fast-forward a few months, and he not only found me an office but a whole suite of offices. He explained that I could sublease several and be rent free. He also arranged with a popular radio station for me to put on a couple of public seminars that each attracted 400-plus people."

"Sounds pretty helpful to me," I added, prematurely.

"Well, that's when it turns ugly—and I mean real ugly," he said. "First off, it turned out that Glenn didn't have any illness at all. Second, we haven't rented out those other offices. And third, I believe he's siphoning off cash from the public seminars that should be going to the radio station. But every time I've brought up any of my suspicions, he's looked at me with accusing eyes and said, 'Are you questioning my integrity?' And each time, I've backed down.

"To complicate the issue," he added, "Glenn has a way of pulling off some really successful stuff, so I wasn't sure if I was just imagining things. But then I found out that the situation was a lot worse than I thought."

To Jerry's horror, he started hearing rumors that Glenn was hitting up people for money, falsely claiming that Jerry would invest it for them. And the week before, Jerry's new car was keyed badly, and the letters of his name were cut off the door of his office.

"Initially, I thought it was some random vandal," Jerry said. "But everything adds up to it being Glenn."

"Do you have any hard evidence?" I asked.

"Nothing I can prove, except that everything points to him. And I know it's him," Jerry replied.

"Have you thought of filing a police report or seeking a restraining order?" I asked.

"Without any hard evidence, I don't think it would work," he said. "Plus, he strikes me as someone who'd just find a way around it. He's pretty ingenious."

"Well, what exactly do you want?" I asked.

"I just want him out of my life."

"Okay," I said. "I think I have a solution for you. First, from what you've told me, it seems that if Glenn is hiding a little, he's hiding a lot, because you can't be just a little bit evil. It's likely that he has a lot of dirty secrets. Second, Glenn has a lot of power over you because he's a sociopath. But he also has one significant vulnerability as a sociopath, and you can exploit it."

I explained that most sociopaths have vivid imaginations. And one way to upset them, and to gain control over them, is to let them know that you're on to them—and on to things they've done to other people as well.

We came up with a game plan and a script. And I agreed to stay in Jerry's consulting room while he went to confront Glenn.

Jerry went into Glenn's office and sat down across from him. "Glenn," he said, "it's come to my attention, thanks to several people I will not name, that you have been doing a number of things to harm me directly and hurt my reputation."

Glenn's face reddened and he yelled back, "Who told you what about me?"

Jerry continued, "I am not going to tell you who they are or what they said. Suffice it to say that I've discovered many things you've done that you thought you hid. You didn't hide them very well. And I'm not the only one who knows."

"You're lying!" Glenn snapped back.

Jerry replied unflinchingly, "If you have nothing to hide, you have nothing to fear. If you have anything to hide, you have everything to fear. And I'm not the only one who knows. Glenn, if you try to do anything further, I will use everything I know about you. I am not a vindictive or retaliatory person, and what I simply want is for you to give me your keys, take all of your belongings, and be out of here in three hours. Otherwise, I will begin to take further action—and that includes asking the police to investigate."

As Jerry got up to leave, Glenn retorted, "I can't be out of here in three hours."

"You can," Jerry said, "and it's not negotiable." He turned on his heel, walked out, and came back into the consulting room, where I was sitting.

As soon as he saw me, he let out a big breath, not believing what he'd just done. Within minutes, we heard Glenn smashing the scenic photos on his office walls. Within two hours, he was gone.

Why can saying, "I know what you're hiding," cause a sociopath to flee from you?

Think about it. What are the odds that you're the first person the sociopath has hurt? And what are the odds that the sociopath has no criminal past? Basically, slim and none. In fact, many sociopaths begin committing evil acts or outright crimes in childhood, so your average sociopath has a long trail of dirty laundry.

Now, put yourself in the head of a sociopath. Your entire life is about doing things that benefit you. So why continue a relationship when you're likely to be exposed and put at risk? That's not your game. You want to mess with other people's lives, not to become a target yourself. So if you feel threatened, you're likely to back off and look for another victim.

In short, the trick in dealing with a sociopath like Glenn isn't to play defense but rather offense, by becoming a threat yourself. This takes considerable courage, but in the long run, it can save you from a monster.

Usable insight •

People who are hiding a little are hiding a lot—and knowing this can give you power over them.

Action Steps

1. If you think you're dealing with a sociopath, study the person carefully over time. Several key characteristics to look for are superficial charm, manipulation, antisocial or risky behavior, and a lack of empathy or remorse.

2. If you determine that you're dealing with a sociopath, do not approach the person without backup. Ask a friend or colleague to be present, either in the room or nearby.

3. Tell the person, "I know what you're hiding." Explain that if the person continues to hurt you, you will take action. Then give the person a specific deadline to get out of your life.

SECTION 4

Eight Ways to Deal with Crazy in Your Personal Life

Up to now, I've focused on tools that work in any setting, professional or personal. In this section, I'll talk specifically about handling the irrational behavior of the most important people in your life: lovers, children, and parents. That's because curing these people's irritating, frustrating, and energy-draining crazy will make you happier at home and more successful and productive in the office.

chapter 22

You've Lost That Lovin' Feeling?

Handling Your Mutual Crazy in a Relationship

ARE YOU IN a marriage or relationship that started out strong but is developing some serious cracks? Then read on, because this chapter is specifically for lovers who don't love each other so much anymore.

While many of my clients these days are in the corporate world, I spent much of my time in earlier years dealing with couples. During this part of my life, I developed an approach I call Recoupling Therapy to help estranged couples regain their love and respect for each other. I have to admit that even I was surprised by how well it worked.

I created Recoupling Therapy primarily to help divorced couples who wanted to get back together, and it involves a great deal of work with a therapist. However, if your relationship is pretty strong but there's significantly more crazy in it than you'd like, there's a do-it-yourself version that can help you make things better.

This is a powerful approach because it doesn't simply encourage you and your partner to treat each other better. It also encourages you to become better people.

First, I'll show you how I've used this approach professionally. After that, I'll teach you the "home" version.

"Hello, Jack," I said over the phone. "This is Dr. Goulston returning your call. How can I help you?"

"My wife, Suzie, and I have been having problems for a long time," Jack began. "We've seen a couple of therapists and we've finally separated, with me moving out into a month-to-month apartment. But now I realize that I don't want a divorce. I'd like to give it another try, and several people said you might be able to help." He added that Suzie also wanted to try again.

I explained to Jack that my approach was highly structured and nonnegotiable. And I added, "I need you and Suzie to be totally on board with how the first 40 minutes will go before I will agree to meet with you."

Jack and Suzie agreed to my terms, so we scheduled a session during which I gave each of them an opportunity to air their complaints. To their credit, they were able to avoid interrupting each other—one of the rules I'd outlined. They also followed my rule about venting part of the time and suggesting solutions for their problems the rest of the time.

When they were done, they looked at me expectantly. Clearly, they assumed that I was eager to discuss their respective grievances in depth.

Instead, I said, "Everything the two of you have said, down to the last word, is . . . irrelevant."

At that point, I could tell that Jack and Suzie were finally in agreement about something: They both thought I was crazy.

Odds are you think I'm crazy, too. After all, I began by specifically asking Jack and Suzie to spell out all of the issues they thought were driving them apart. And then I told them that I couldn't care less about those issues. People don't expect a psychiatrist to say something like that.

However, I was making an important point. It wasn't their actions that made their relationship toxic. It was their personalities.

Looking at the two of them, I said, "I want to ask you if you agree with something. Can I proceed?"

"Uhhh, yeah," said Frank.

"Okay," said Suzie, who seemed even less enthused.

First, I showed them a sketch (see Figure 22–1).

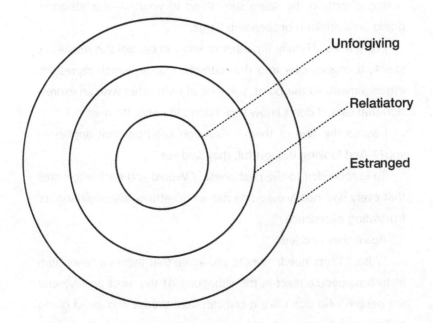

FIGURE 22–1: Negative Personality Traits in a Relationship

Then I said, "People's negative personality traits in a relationship fall into three concentric circles. The innermost circle represents our unforgiving streak. This is what gets triggered when someone upsets or frustrates us. Everybody has an unforgiving streak—even Mother Teresa had one. If we don't keep this streak under control, we can become 100 percent unforgiving. That is what bitter people are: 100 percent unforgiving. Do you each know someone like that?"

They nodded.

"Not very fun to be around, right?"

They nodded again.

I went on, "If your unforgiving streak overtakes you, it overflows and crosses over into the next outer circle, which houses your retaliatory streak. When that happens, you focus on getting back at the person you feel has offended you. You do this either by hurting the person directly or by doing something to yourself—for instance, going on a drinking or spending binge."

I continued, "Finally, if neither of you can control this retaliatory streak, it crosses over into the outermost circle, which represents estrangement. At this point, you look at each other with an expression that says, 'I don't know you. I don't like you. It's over.'"

I asked the two of them, "Can you see how that applies to you?" And looking thoughtful, they said yes.

So I proceeded to the next phase. "Would you each also agree that every day, nearly everyone has an upsetting, disappointing, or frustrating experience?"

Again they nodded.

"Also," I continued, "would you agree that there's a continuum as to how people react in this situation? At the most positive end are people who don't like it but can take the hit and avoid going ballistic at someone else or beating up on themselves. They show poise under pressure, and we admire them and would like to be like them. Agreed?"

They said yes.

"On the most negative end," I went on, "are people who treat the slightest inconvenience or upset as a major catastrophe and scream at others or mercilessly beat up on themselves. These are the people we least like, least want to be around, and least want to be like. That's because they're infantile, and we find their actions repulsive."

Again, they nodded.

"Now here is where all of this applies to the two of you," I said. "In the context of your relationship, both of you are like addicts.

You're addicted to reacting to upsets in an infantile, repulsive way. Your behavior is unforgiving. It's retaliatory. And it's why you became estranged, could no longer stand to be around each other, and split. Make sense?"

"Yes," they replied.

They saw the problem. Now we just needed to solve it. And I knew how.

"From this day forward," I told them, "I want you to become *sponsors* for each other."

Each day, I explained, they would work on developing emotional toughness and the ability to handle upsets, frustrations, and disappointments without going off the deep end. They'd practice taking the hit and dealing with it more maturely. I outlined strategies for taking hits with poise (which, by the way, are the same strategies I discussed in Section 2).

Then I got to the heart of the matter.

"I want you to keep track of each situation in which you triumph over your negative emotions. Maybe you stop yourself from yelling at your kids when they're whining in the car. Maybe you stay calm instead of screaming at someone at work who makes a careless error. Or maybe you're very patient with a difficult parent.

"Then you're going to share your triumphs with each other at the end of the day. And if you have setbacks, you can share those as well because your partner isn't your enemy anymore. Your partner is now your sponsor."

Jack and Suzie did what I asked. It wasn't easy, and sometimes they backslid. But over the next few months, a remarkable thing happened. Instead of harping on each other's shortcomings, they started telling me how much they respected each other. They started looking at each other, smiling at each other, and touching each other in the way that people who are in love do.

And a year later, they renewed their wedding vows.

Over the course of my early years as a psychiatrist, I used this approach with many couples who were divorced or separated and wanted to get back together. And here's what I found:

▶ After 6 weeks, many of these couples said their relationship was better than ever.

▶ After 12 weeks, many said they were better as individuals than they ever had been.

▶ After 18 weeks, many commented that other people were asking them what had happened. In one case, the couple chuckled and replied, "We decided to grow up."

Why does this approach work so well? Because it gives each partner something to aspire to. As long as both people are involved in deal making, they're still focused on either getting their way or reaching a compromise. With this approach, they transcend the transactional and become people who are better than either of them thought was possible—people they are proud to be.

On top of it all, the two people help each other achieve this remarkable goal. They cheer each other on. They offer each other pats on the back, and they keep each other committed. In the process, they begin loving and respecting each other again.

Now, in a very broken relationship, this process can be highly challenging. So if your relationship is seriously damaged, or you're already separated or divorced, you should seek the assistance of a professional counselor. However, if you love each other deeply, and your relationship is fundamentally strong but you sense that you're both falling into crazy (or you're already there), you can use this approach on your own. I like to call this simpler version Happily Ever After because that's an achievable goal—if you're willing to work hard at it.

The key to this approach is recognizing that both your partner and you are responsible for the problems you're experiencing. To succeed, you both need to feel contrite about the mistakes you've made, not just frustrated with each other. And if you have children, you both need to recognize that your bad behavior and selfishness are harming them, too.

If you're able to admit these things, and your partner can accept personal responsibility as well, then give my approach a try:

1. Sit down with your partner. Say, "There's something I'd like to try to make our relationship even stronger. And I think it will help make us even better people."

2. Talk about how you want to become better at handling upsets, frustrations, and disappointments so you don't become unforgiving, retaliatory, or estranged.

3. Ask if your partner is willing to sponsor you in your effort. Then ask if you can act as a sponsor in return. If your partner agrees, make a firm mutual commitment to work on becoming better people.

4. Every day, spend time reporting to each other on your triumphs and setbacks. And in your roles as sponsors, offer moral support and acknowledge progress.

I think you'll be surprised at how much you grow, both as a partner and as a person, when you try this. And I'm betting that your partner will grow as well. That's because inside most people who are acting immaturely is a desire to rise above it and be the people they're capable of being. They have a will. All they need is a way. This is that way.

Usable insight ●●●●●●●●●●●●●●●●●●●●●●●●●

When you and your partner help each other become the best you can be, you stop being the worst you can be.

Action Steps

1. Analyze your relationship with your partner. Are you supportive of each other? Do you respect each other? Do you spend more time laughing than fighting? Do you look

forward to seeing your partner at the end of the day, or do you increasingly dread coming home? If you have children, what are they learning—good or bad—from your relationship with your partner?

2. If you don't like your answers to these questions, fully acknowledge your own failings in your relationship. In addition, acknowledge the pain those failings have caused your partner and other people in your family.

3. Then ask if your partner would like to work with you so you both can become saner and better partners—and saner and better people.

chapter 23

Shock
Absorber

Getting Through to
an Emotional Partner

DOES THIS sound like your life?

You come home exhausted after work, and all you want is a little quiet—and maybe, if you're lucky, a little affection. But instead, your partner lights into you as soon as you get in the door: "Do you know what your daughter did at school today? She humiliated me in front of the PTA president. When I offered to make something for the bake sale, she said, 'I'll bet people would pay *not* to eat my mom's crappy gluten-free cookies.' After everything I do to make sure she eats right, she embarrasses me about it."

You see yourself as the calm person in your relationship and your partner as the irrational one. So when your partner starts yelling, you see yourself as a human sedative.

That's why you say something like, "Okay, okay, it's all right, calm down. It was just a joke."

Or you say, "I know she mouths off sometimes, but hey, underneath that attitude she's a good kid."

Or you say, "Hey, I had a bad day, too, but it's over, so let's relax and talk about something else."

And that's when all hell breaks loose. Because guess what: You didn't pour baking soda on the fire. You poured lighter fluid on it.

"Calm down?" your partner says. "That's easy for you to say. She doesn't pull crap like this on you because she hardly even knows you. *I* don't even know you. That's because you're married to your job. And furthermore, where is that milk I asked you to pick up on your way home from work? Don't you listen to anything I say?"

What's happening here? You're being calm, sensible, and rational. And you're totally screwing up. Your partner doesn't need a human sedative right now. Your partner needs a human shock absorber. Just ask Ben, who learned this lesson the hard way.

"When I think of my marriage, it's *Bambi* meets *Groundhog Day*," Ben told me.

"What do you mean?" I asked.

"Nearly every day when I leave work, I feel like a cute little baby deer, romping through the forest and looking forward to seeing my family. And then *wham*! Angie hits me with a shotgun blast about something I did wrong or says, 'We've got a problem!' It happens in seconds—almost like she can't wait to lay into me. I don't even have a chance to take my jacket off."

"What happens after that?" I asked.

"I try to calm her down, but that just makes her go ballistic."

"Tell me a little about Angie," I said.

"She's actually terrific," said Ben. "I'd be lost without her. She works and she also handles most of what goes on in our house. That includes dealing with our 8-year-old son, Jack, who has severe autism. And it includes taking care of our 12-year-old daughter, Abby, who's easier to manage but still a handful. Angie is a control freak and a bit of a perfectionist, and the kids drive her crazy."

Ben told me that Angie's parents divorced when she was 11. "Her dad is pretty much out of the picture now, but her mom is always criticizing her. Angie feels like she can't ever please her."

"Do you think Angie got her critical and perfectionistic nature from her mom?" I asked.

"Absolutely," he said. "But to Angie's credit, she can't stand those qualities in herself. However, when she's stressed—and Jack does that to her every day—her worst side comes out."

I looked Ben straight in the eye and asked, "Do you think Angie ever wished that Jack had never been born, or even worse, that he were out of her life, maybe permanently?"

"Whoa!" Ben blurted out. He looked shocked, but he was quiet for a minute.

Then he said, "I guess she's sort of hinted once or twice on really bad days that she wished he'd never been born. But I've never heard her say the rest of it."

"So she's never told you that she wished Jack was dead?" I asked.

"That's crazy! No, of course not! How could you suggest such a thing?" Ben said, alarmed by my question.

"Because when we're under a huge stress, as controlling, perfectionistic Angie is when she's dealing with Jack acting at his worst, we become distressed," I said. "And when we become distressed, our lower brain takes over and all we can think about is escaping."

I asked Ben if Angie dealt with Jack's behaviors, or her own anger about those behaviors, by giving Jack or herself a time-out.

"Wow, that's exactly what she does. How did you know that?" Ben asked.

"Simple," I said. "As you said, Angie's a good person and doesn't want to be like her mother. When Jack pushes her buttons, she needs to do something physically to prevent herself from becoming cruel or maybe even abusive. That's why she knows that either Jack or she needs a time-out.

"Similarly, she needs to do something emotionally to prevent herself from thinking cruel thoughts. That's where you come in, Bambi."

"What do you mean?" Ben asked.

"If Angie's unconscious mind is saying to her, 'The only way for this problem to be over is for Jack to die,' she can't possibly allow herself to feel such a thought. So she takes it out on you, which explains why nothing you say or do makes it better. That's because the issue isn't about you. The issue is Angie wanting to get away from thoughts and feelings that would cause her to feel horrible about herself."

Ben's eyes began to tear up. "Wow. It all makes sense now," he said. "What can I do?"

"There's an awkward term in psychology called *mediated catharsis*," I said. "It means feeling some of the awful feelings she's feeling and talking with her about them. For instance, you can say, 'Angie, do you ever hate Jack and wish he was gone from our lives and your life? Because if I were you, I think I might think that a lot. In fact, I think if I didn't have you dealing with him, I might think that myself, and it's a devastating thought.' Saying that will help her feel less alone and less like an awful person."

On a practical level, I also told Ben that he needed to reduce Angie's stress by taking on more of the load at home. "Don't wait for her to tell you," I said, "because that will just stress her out more."

Ben tried my suggestions. And while things aren't always totally peaceful when he comes home, they're way, way better now. Most nights Ben gets a "Hi" or even a hug from Angie when he gets home—not a shotgun blast.

Mediated catharsis will work with any emotional person who needs to vent. But it's an especially good choice if you're dealing with a partner who's taking care of demanding young children or antagonistic teens, or one who's handling the responsibility of caring for an aging parent. Here's why:

▸ As parents, we believe we need to love our children every moment. As a result, when children do truly awful things (as all kids do sometimes), parents are scared by the hostile thoughts they have toward their kids. So they redirect their negative feelings toward a safer target. In this case, that's you.

▶ Most people feel they need to love their parents unconditionally. So if they think unthinkable thoughts about those
parents—"Dealing with her cancer is so awful, I wish she
would just die"—you'll have a target on your back.

In shrink terms, this is called displacement. When my patients
are terrified of expressing anger toward their mothers, fathers, or
children—or if they're in any other situation in which their own
emotions are too scary to confront—they attack me. That's because
it's safe. And because I know what's going on, I'm fine with that.

Right now, you're in the same position. And the human sedative approach isn't going to cut it. Instead, you should do what Ben
learned to do: Be a human shock absorber.

Usable insight •

When good and loving people feel overwhelmed by intolerable hateful and cruel thoughts, they will do anything to get
away from them, including taking aim at you.

Action Steps

1. Think of someone who's acting in an overly negative, critical, or hostile manner toward you.

2. If the person is dyed-in-the-wool hurtful, cruel, and mean,
   get away from her.

3. However, if you suspect that the person is acting in a negative way because of overwhelming feelings she can't safely
   express, put yourself in her shoes. Say, "If I were you having to deal with this, I would be at my wits' end and maybe
   even want to do something really destructive. Do you ever
   feel that way?"

Important note: If you're not ready for an honest answer,
don't ask the question.

• ▬

chapter 24

Copy Cat

Getting a Strong-and-Silent
Partner to Talk

SO FAR, the techniques I've described in this book are pretty intense and often involve some serious forms of crazy. But just for a minute, let's have some fun.

Here's a little trick I teach spouses or lovers who are living with emotionally "constipated" people who become resentful when their partners try to talk with them about their emotions. While we all like these strong, silent types in movies, they can drive their spouses or lovers nuts in real life. And in reality, their refusal to discuss their problems is irrational, because over time, it turns small issues into giant ones.

Luckily, there's a quick, sassy trick for snapping these people out of their silent treatment. Here's how one of my clients used it.

Della came to my office to talk about some serious problems she was having with her mom. But in passing, we got to talking about her husband, Eric. He was a great guy, she said, but sometimes he annoyed the heck out of her.

"He'll come home all tense," she said, "but when I ask what's wrong, he'll just clam up and say, 'Nothing,' and walk away.

Sometimes I wind up following him around the house saying, 'Talk to me!' or 'Listen to me!' But that doesn't work either, because he just escapes into the bathroom or even heads out the door."

I laughed. "You've just described a quarter of the marriages in America," I said. "But if you're tired of this routine, I have a little trick you can try."

A few days later, Eric came home radiating stress. "Bad day?" Della asked.

"Mmmmm," he mumbled, heading straight for the TV.

Della said to herself: "Game on."

She let him play with the remote for a while. Then she sat down across from him and said in a firm but positive tone, "I'd like your help with something."

Eric said, "What?" in an exasperated tone.

"I'd like you to look me directly in the eye and say exactly what I say, without thinking about it."

"What?" Eric repeated. But Della persisted, and he could tell she wasn't going to leave him alone until he agreed. So he grudgingly said, "Okay."

Then Della looked him in the eye and said, "Get off my f#@&ing back. Talking about it doesn't make me feel any better. Just shut the f#@& up."

Eric's mouth fell open. But Della gestured at him: Say it. So he did.

Della could see that he was shocked and totally disarmed, but also curious about what would happen next.

Then Della simply smiled sweetly and said, "Good. Now you're talking!" And then she added, "I figured that's what you wanted to get off your chest. So—what should we have for dinner?"

Eric shook his head and laughed, feeling like he'd just dumped a huge load on Della without making anything worse.

"You're nuts," he said.

And then he thought for a minute.

And he said, "Okay, I guess I am hard to talk to."

This little "crazy hack" often gets a withdrawn person to open up because it allows him to confront you in a hostile way, and—in the process—blow off a big load of resentment. It's a little like the A-E-U technique I described in Chapter 9, but by getting the person to say the words, you provide an even greater catharsis. And it allows you to empathize with the person's feelings, which makes him more willing to empathize with you.

Best of all, this trick is fun, and it can put your partner in an entirely different mood. Frequently, in fact, the next move won't be dinner . . . but bed. And that's where Della and Eric wound up.

Usable insight •

Do unto yourself what others would like to do . . . but won't, because it's too rude.

Action Steps

1. Wait for a night when you and your partner are alone.

2. Get your partner to repeat your copycat sentence.

3. Move on, immediately, to another everyday topic, to signal that everything is fine.

• ▬▬▬▬

chapter 25

Child A
or Child B?

Going Through a Divorce
Without Wrecking
Your Kids for Life

DIVORCE IS brutal, and when kids are involved, it's doubly so. As a psychiatrist, I've spent way too many hours of my life listening to divorcing parents screaming at each other about who loves the kids more, who's screwed them up the most, and who's getting them on Thanksgiving Day.

Unfortunately, these shouting matches don't just happen in a shrink's or a lawyer's office; they also happen at home. And when kids overhear these battles—especially when parents keep screaming about the same issues without ever resolving anything—it can traumatize them in lasting ways. I know, because I hear about it decades later.

If you and your partner are heading for a divorce (or you're already in the throes of one), I know how hard it is to avoid bare-knuckle fights over the kids. That's especially true if your partner keeps ruthlessly pushing your parental buttons. And frankly, if you want to fight in private, or save your attacks for your therapist's or lawyer's office, that's fine with me.

But when it comes to your kids, you have a bigger responsibility: to ensure that your divorce damages them as little as possible. That means that you need to behave in a cooperative, respectful way toward each other when your child is around. And it means that rather than focusing on your current grievances, you both need to focus on your child's future.

The best method I know for accomplishing these goals is an approach based on the Going Forward technique I described in Chapter 1. I call it Child A or Child B? Here's how it works.

Elena and Sam came to my office because they realized that their scorched-earth approach to their divorce was hurting them and their daughter, Grace. But even though they knew this, they couldn't stop attacking each other.

"You buy her crap, like all that makeup, so she'll take your side," Elena started in. "She's 12 and she looks like a hooker, but you don't care as long as she loves you more."

"She's a teenager and you're treating her like a baby," he yelled in return. "It's no wonder she's a mess. Just because you're a f#@&ing prude doesn't mean you have to turn her into one."

I let them bash away at each other like this for a while. But then I asked them to stop for a minute because I had a question for them. "Which child do you want to have 10 years from now?" I asked. "Child A or Child B?"

They both said, "What?"

"Child A or Child B?" I repeated.

They stared at me, confused.

"Here's the difference," I explained. And I sketched out this chart on a piece of paper:

CHILD A	CHILD B
Focused	Scattered
Resilient	Fragile
Persistent	Quits when things get tough

Goal oriented	Lacking goals
Able to handle disappointments in a mature way	Easily upset
Doesn't take herself too seriously	Hypersensitive
Willing to listen to other people's advice and learn from it	Unable to take advice without going ballistic

They both made the obvious choice: Child A.

"Then here's the deal," I said. "While you may not believe it, the relationship between the two of you is far more important to Grace right now than how you act toward her. And your relationship doesn't just affect how she feels right now. It will be the model for how she's going to behave, what she's going to believe, and who she's going to be for the rest of her life.

"And right now, you're creating Child B."

At this point, seeing expressions of pain cross their faces, I could tell I was getting through to them.

"Here are the three things I want you to think about," I said. "First, are you both agreed that Grace will have a better life if she turns out to be Child A?"

They nodded.

"Second, do you both understand that you have a moral obligation to do right by Grace, and that this means focusing on her future rather than your current grievances, and resolving your issues in a cooperative, mutually respectful way?"

They hesitated—because they weren't quite ready to abandon their grudges—but again, they nodded.

"Then here's step three," I said. "Going forward, I don't want to hear about what's best for either of you right now, or even what you think is best for Grace right now. Instead, I want you each to make a compelling and convincing case for what you're asking for regarding living arrangements, custody, and coparenting, and explain how it will result in Grace becoming Child A rather than Child B. If you can't make such a case for your request, I will dismiss it as irrelevant."

I won't say that Elena and Sam stopped sniping at each other entirely after that, but they did a far better job of hashing things out civilly in my office, and they worked even harder to behave at home around Grace. And when one of them did go on the attack, the other would simply say quietly, "A or B?" Generally, that was enough to get them back on track, because now they understood the high stakes they were playing for.

While this approach is easy to describe on paper, I know that it's infinitely harder to carry out in real life. A divorce is one of the most wrenching experiences you can go through, and it's tough to keep from falling into constant amygdala hijack. And even if you're able to keep your own emotions under control and put your child's future first, your partner might not be willing to do the same.

But do your best. Explain to your partner that your mutual actions during this awful time in your lives will powerfully affect your child's future well-being. Say that you are going to do the following two things, and see if your partner will agree to them as well:

▶ You will behave in a respectful and cooperative way toward your partner.

▶ You will make decisions based on the goal of having your child turn out like Child A rather than Child B.

Stick by these rules whether your partner does or not. If you feel yourself melting down, practice the drills I outlined in Chapter 6 for keeping your own crazy at bay. And if you do lose it, do the drills I described in Chapter 7 for regrouping.

Oh, and one more thing. Even though you're acting nobly and doing what's best for your child, don't expect your child to appreciate this. Right now, your child is sad, scared, angry, and very irrational—with good reason. You're likely to hear things like, "I hate you," or, "I will never forgive you." That's especially true if your partner tries to sabotage your relationship with your child by saying nasty things about you.

If that happens—tough. Keep doing what you're doing, no matter what.

Remember, you're playing the long game, not the short game. And what's at stake is your child's life. That's more important than your feelings, and it's even more important than whether your child loves you right now or not.

By the way, here's a secret I've learned from three decades as a therapist. During a divorce, a child frequently sides with the crazier parent. (That's because this parent is the most likely to play dirty and use bribes.) But looking back later in life, the child virtually always sees through that parent's tricks and grows to appreciate the actions of the saner parent.

So no matter how awful things get, keep thinking about Child A. When you do this, you and your child will win in the end. And if you and your partner can stay focused on Child A, you'll all win, which is the best possible way for a divorce to end.

Usable insight

If you're going through a divorce, let go of focusing on your own need to be right and instead focus on what's right for your child.

Action Steps

1. If you're in the process of getting a divorce (or you're already divorced but still feuding with your ex), reread my descriptions of Child A and Child B.

2. Decide if you care more about your child's future than you do about your own need to be right and your need to be loved by your child right now.

3. If the answer is yes, make these two resolutions and stick to them whether or not your partner agrees:

> ▸ You will behave in a respectful and cooperative way toward your partner.

> ▸ You will make decisions based on the goal of having your child turn out like Child A rather than Child B.

chapter 26

"What's the Worst Thing for You?"

Being There for a Parent, Partner, or Child in Pain

FREQUENTLY, we try to play Pollyanna when our loved ones are upset. We say things like, "It'll be fine," or, "You're luckier than most people," or, "Think of all the good things in your life."

Sometimes that's okay. But often, it doesn't make people feel better. Instead, it makes them feel unheard. That's because instead of acknowledging their pain, we're ignoring or trivializing it. And this can transform people from slightly crazy into really crazy.

So rather than glossing over the pain of people who are feeling highly emotional or afraid or hopeless, your best approach may be to head straight for it. Rather than trying to get these people to think about the best parts of their lives, get them to talk about the worst.

I know this sounds strange, or even cruel. But it's actually very kind, and it works. Here's how I used it recently to help some kids who were really hurting.

What do you say to a group of homeless 10- to 17-year-olds living with their single mothers at one of the largest homeless shelters in the country, in one of the most drug- and crime-infested parts of Los Angeles?

That was my challenge when entrepreneur Christopher Kai asked me to come speak at Mondays at the Mission at the Union Rescue Mission. "You'll be great with these kids," he said. "Just do something to inspire them."

I wasn't sure I could. But in retrospect, I think—just maybe—I did.

Driving through Skid Row triggered flashbacks of my visits to Mumbai and Delhi years before. Each homeless person I saw in Los Angeles was trying to stake out a few square feet of space, which was marked by an unfolded sleeping bag or maybe a shopping cart.

As I entered the Union Rescue Mission, it seemed like a fragile oasis in the middle of a nightmare. Walking down a corridor to the rec room where I was scheduled to speak, I saw single mothers corralling their children so they wouldn't wander too far. Night was approaching; danger was everywhere.

Before my talk, Chris, who founded the Mondays at the Mission program, came in to deliver a brief orientation. As he spoke, I quietly looked out over the kids in the room and felt the fear, pain, and sadness behind their quiet faces. I knew there was a lot of crazy in their lives, and it had to be making them feel crazy at times.

Because I also knew that I needed to address these kids' emotions, after introducing myself I told them to pair up and look into each other's eyes (much like the Fishbowl technique I described in Chapter 13). Then I instructed one child in each pair to answer the following question in one sentence and one sentence only: "What's the toughest thing about your life right now?"

When asked this question, some of the children began to cry. The volunteers and I stepped in to reinforce that it was okay to cry and safe to speak up, whereupon several teenagers answered emotionally, "Being here."

Immediately, I felt the room shift into a different energy—calmer, kinder, and more caring. These kids, who five minutes ago had felt alone in their pain, now felt heard.

Then I told the children they had a homework assignment. "When I first walked into the room, I saw that many of your moms seemed upset or tense. Now that you've practiced this exercise in here, I want you to try it with them, but not immediately. Pick a quiet time when you're with your mom and say to her, 'Mom, what's the toughest part of being here for you?'"

I added, "Some of your mothers will start crying because they're afraid and ashamed of being here. Crying will be good for them and good for you. Don't get nervous, because you're actually showing them your love. I want you to let your moms cry and then reach out and hug them and say, 'It's okay, Mom. We're going to be okay and I love you.'"

That made nearly everyone in the room tear up. And I knew that many of these kids would have amazing conversations with their moms—and maybe change those moms' lives forever.

This simple question—What's the worst thing for you right now?—can be life altering because it makes people feel less alone.

Pain is pain. But suffering is feeling alone in pain. When you take away the aloneness, the suffering that people can't endure becomes pain they can withstand. As a result, people who've been acting out their pain by crying, yelling, or withdrawing can deal with it in a saner way.

That's why this one question can lead to a huge breakthrough in your relationship with a spouse or lover. In addition, it can lead to amazing conversations with your parents.

And here's where it's really dynamite: when you're dealing with an irrational teen.

In Chapter 2, I mentioned how we make the journey from separation anxiety to individuation anxiety early in life. On paper, this sounds simple. But in real life, the psychological terrain between dependence and independence is fraught with anxiety, confusion, and fear. Navigating it successfully requires teenagers to let go of dependence on their parents. The more they need their parents, the less independent and more ashamed they feel. This shame causes irritability, leading them to snap at their parents.

As kids wander through this stormy, scary landscape, they often feel a deeply painful and dark despair. To adults, this may seem like nothing more than teenage angst. But it's not. As children break the ties with the people who used to be their entire world, despair is really des-pair: a feeling of being unpaired in a world where everyone else seems to be paired with hope rather than hopelessness, meaning rather than meaninglessness, worth rather than worthlessness, and a point to living rather than pointlessness.

What's the cure for a child trapped in this transition? What hopeless, helpless, meaningless, worthless, and pointless have in common is "less"—as in without hope, help, meaning, worth, or a point to go on. The key to helping a teen who feels this way is to give this child a "with" experience.

And here's where asking, "What's the worst thing for you?" can make a world of difference. This question tells your teen, "You're not alone. I'm here with you."

Realize, however, that when you ask this question, your goal isn't to try to fix your child's problems or take control of the situation. This will just make a child who's inching toward independence feel ashamed and angry. Instead, your goal is to simply be with your child.

Wait until you're sure you can keep your own "solvaholic" instincts under control. Then, in some quiet moment when your teen is acting less crazy than usual, do the following:

▸ Say, "I would like to understand something better. Would it be okay if I asked you a question?" This gives your child the chance to shift from emotional reactivity (every teen's M.O.) to possibly listening to you. If your teen refuses, calmly say, "That's okay. It can wait, or we can just let it go." But most likely, your child's need to be in control of any conversation with you will cause her to sigh in an aggrieved way and say, "Okay. Fine. What is it?" Say, "What's the worst thing in your life right now?" When you say this, your teen may look at you in a perplexed way and, being off balance, may even respond, "What?" If that happens, just repeat the question.

▶ If your teen offers an answer, go deeper. Ask, "At its worst, how bad does that get for you?" When you say this, your child may begin to tear up because your inviting tone is helping her to feel less alone. These are healing tears; don't try to stop them. Allow your child to respond and then say, "And when it's at its worst, what does it make you want to do?" At this point, your child may say something like "give up" or "crawl in a hole and die." If so, don't react with anxiety or a solution. If you do that, it's like offering your child an invitation to open up and then immediately slamming the door. Instead say, "Look into my eyes." Then say, "I didn't know it was so bad, and I apologize if I caused you to feel that I didn't want to know. I want to help, but I may need your help because I'm a solvaholic, and a solution is not what you need right now. I think what you need is to feel less alone. And you need to know that it's going to get better."

When you use this approach with a child—or with anyone in your family who's feeling alone, afraid, or hopeless—don't expect it to solve everything. After all, the problems the person is dealing with will still be there. But by letting her know she isn't alone in facing those problems, you'll turn unbearable suffering into bearable pain. And that can give the person the strength to say, "I can handle this."

Usable insight •

If you want someone to open up, try a bait-and-stay.

Action Steps

1. If someone in your family is battling big issues—whether it's a parent dealing with cancer, a spouse who's out of work, or a teen who's angry or withdrawn—find a quiet time and ask, "What's the worst thing for you?"

2. When the person answers, extend the conversation with additional questions or say, "Tell me more." The longer you talk, the less alone the person will feel.

3. Depending on the situation, consider working together on a plan of action to move the person from despondent to hopeful.

chapter 27

The Reconnect

Healing a Broken Relationship
with an Adult Child

ONE OF THE saddest experiences in life is to be the mother or father of a child who refuses to have anything to do with you. It's called parental alienation syndrome, and it's far more common than you'd think.

Sometimes, of course, adult children disconnect for sane and valid reasons. For instance, their parents may be abusive, self-destructive, or otherwise toxic. In cases like this, walking away is sometimes a child's only good choice.

If you went through a temporary destructive or self-destructive phase that cost you a relationship with a child—for instance, if you were addicted to drugs or alcohol or behaved horribly during a divorce—there's a way to rehabilitate that relationship. I cover it in Chapter 29. It's not easy, and there's no guarantee that it will work, but I think you'll feel better if you try it.

Right now, however, I want to discuss a different kind of alienation, the kind that isn't a parent's fault. Surprisingly, I see this scenario a lot. In it, kids blame their parents for their messed-up lives for a very specific reason: They can't blame themselves.

Sound crazy? Yeah, it is.

A few weeks ago, I ran into an acquaintance of mine. He looked really down, so I asked him why. (Hey, I'm a shrink. We meddle.)

He said, "My oldest daughter, Angie, hasn't spoken to me for a year and a half. My middle daughter, Dru, talked to her this week, and Angie told her, 'I never want to speak to him again.'"

As I talked more with my friend, it became clear that he hadn't done anything horrible or unforgivable to Angie. In fact, he'd treated her in pretty much the same way as his other kids, who still adored him.

It's true that he hadn't always been as supportive as possible, but not every parent can be perfect every day. And sometimes he'd "checked out" when his children needed him, but even nice parents can sometimes do that when their kids' problems overwhelm them. What's more, as a corporate CEO, he'd had a lot on his plate. Anyone who's held that job knows it's all too easy to shortchange your family when the pressure mounts at the office.

My friend's sins were clearly venial, not mortal. And that made it easy for me to guess what was happening.

"Do you want to know what's really going on here?" I asked.

My friend said yes. So I explained that his daughter needed to hate him because she had a rigid personality.

People with rigid personalities come in different flavors. Some are inflexible but pretty typical otherwise. Some are perfectionists who expect others to be perfect as well. Some fall on the mild end of the autism spectrum. And some have borderline personality disorders.

Here's what all of these people have in common: They can't adapt to new situations because they aren't flexible enough. And because they can't adapt, they get into trouble.

However, when something goes wrong, these people don't want to admit that it's their fault. That would be like saying, "I can't fix this." Being stuck forever with no way out is a very scary feeling.

As a result, rigid people have a great need to not be wrong, because if they are, and they're too rigid to fix it, they're left feeling powerless and helpless. So at the first sign of a challenge they won't be able to handle, these people grab on to someone else to blame. And typically, that someone else is Mom or Dad. I was pretty sure that was the story in this case.

My friend asked what he could do. I told him to ask his middle daughter, Dru, to pass on a message from him. In it, I said, he should apologize for his failings and, more important, open the door to reconciliation. Based on my advice, here's what he wrote:

> I'm asking Dru to give you this message. And if you don't want to read it, it's okay.
>
> I want to apologize for two things. First, I really don't understand you. And second, even though I should have tried harder to understand you, I've been afraid to. That's because I tend to steer clear of things that overwhelm me.
>
> If you feel like I've abandoned you, you're right. But here is what I want you to know. I am open to any conversation, and any ideas about how to fix this, for as long as I live.

When he read his note to me, my friend teared up. "It's weird because what you said is so right," he told me.

He explained that he'd indeed felt overwhelmed and frightened when his kids had emotional problems. His other children, who were more self-reliant than Angie, coped by solving their problems on their own or with the help of their mom; and later, when they married, they shared their problems with their spouses. But Angie, who couldn't solve her problems on her own and didn't have a partner, had no one to blame but him.

In reality, what Angie mistook for abandonment wasn't that at all. It was fear. And my friend was willing to face that fear and work at being there for Angie in the future if there was a chance that he could get his daughter back.

I talked to my friend recently, and he gave me an update. When Dru forwarded his note to Angie, she replied, "Okay. Fine. I'll talk with him. But we're not going to talk about this note." Angie was ready to open the door—just a crack—to reconciliation. But she wanted to do it on her terms, rather than having her dad think that she was obeying his request.

I'm hopeful that in this case, my strategy will work out over time. However, here's a caution: Don't assume that it will work, even a little bit, every time. When children are totally stuck in their rigidity, especially if they have borderline personalities, they may not be able to give up their blame game.

But even when this approach doesn't bring parents and children back together, it helps the parents heal. That's because the people who reach out feel they've been as honest as they can be and they've done as much as they can. So even when they don't achieve victory, they experience the relief of closure.

Usable insight ●●●●●●●●●●●●●●●●●●●●●●●●●●

If a child hates you for no obvious reason, ask yourself if that hatred is covering up a fear of being wrong or, worse, a fear of being crazy.

Action Steps

1. If a child you love isn't speaking to you, find a willing intermediary. (Make sure it's someone who's okay with this job.)

2. Compose a letter like the one I've outlined and send it. In it, admit to your shortcomings as a parent.

3. Realize that if the person does reconnect with you, you'll need to work on being more supportive yourself. And realize that if the person won't reconnect, you've done all you can.

●●●

chapter 28

The Assumptive Close

Getting an Aging Parent
to Accept Help

ASK ANY ADULT child: There is no one—no one—more crazy or crazy making than a parent who's aging badly.

However, I can sympathize with old people who are acting irrationally. (And not just because I'm inching closer to old age myself.) Imagine what it's like to go from being the respected or even feared matriarch or patriarch of your family to being the person everyone treats like a child. Or picture what it's like to go from being a high-powered doctor, accountant, or corporate manager to being a frail senior with liver spots and too much nose hair.

Now imagine losing even more control. Having to give up driving. Needing a walker. Needing to wear adult diapers. Needing help to fix dinner—or even to go to the bathroom. Imagine feeling your control over your mind, your body, and your life slipping away day by day.

Then, worse yet, imagine your child—the infant whose bottom you wiped, the teen you taught to drive, the young adult you guided—having to drive you to the store, fix your meals, handle your finances, and yes, possibly even clean up your bathroom messes.

When you think about it, it's no wonder that so many aging people are miserable. And it's no wonder that they make their adult children miserable as well. Because the only thing that's worse than losing your abilities is reversing roles with your son or daughter— becoming dependent on the person who used to depend on you.

When Jen's father reached his 80s, he refused to move in with her or go to a nursing home. She hired home healthcare aides for him, but he managed to drive every one of them away within weeks. So every few days, Jen made the hour-long drive to his house to bring him food, do his laundry, mow his lawn, mop his floors, and wash his dishes.

Jen could manage that, but what really upset her was that her dad refused to give up driving. His neighbors, who constantly worried about their children's safety, finally took matters into their own hands by slashing his tires and disconnecting his battery one night when he left the car unlocked. (And Jen, who knew the neighbors were behind the vandalism, silently said, "Thank you.")

Even after that, every day was a crapshoot for Jen. Sometimes she'd make it through the day without a crisis. Other days, her dad's neighbors would call to report that he'd fallen when he was trying to rake the yard or take out the trash. Or the emergency room would call when a relative found him in a diabetic coma because he'd forgotten to take his insulin shots. Or he'd call her house at 2 a.m., confused and asking why she wasn't there to take him to a doctor's appointment that was scheduled for 10 a.m.

But still, he insisted that he was fine on his own, no matter how much evidence to the contrary mounted.

"Last Christmas was the worst," Jen told me. "I planned to pick him up early so he could spend the whole day at our house. But at 9 a.m., he called and said, 'I fell in the living room, but I'll be fine here on the floor for now. Don't worry; just go ahead without me.'" Needless to say, she didn't—and it turned out to be another very long day in the emergency room.

If you're lucky, and your mom and dad are still physically and mentally fit and reasonably sane, you can prevent this kind of situation by addressing it before it arises. For instance, you can sit your parents down and say, "We're lucky because right now you aren't facing any medical issues, and you're totally independent. So let's talk about things now, when we don't have to." Then, if they agree, you can talk together about what their wishes are for that hopefully distant future in which they can no longer care for themselves. Better yet, you may be able to get them to spell out their desires in writing.

However, not all parents will agree to this. In fact, your mother or father may adamantly refuse, or simply stall you—forever. And if that happens, you'll eventually wind up being held hostage by your parent's denial.

Elderly parents frequently can't admit they need help because with each admission, they lose more of themselves. Ironically, by refusing to accept a reasonable level of help—a move to your home or an assisted-care facility, a cab ride to the grocery store, a nursing aide, or a housekeeper—these people end up needing more help. In effect, they're becoming less capable and more of a problem. But they can't see this because they're trapped in their own kind of crazy.

What can you do to get through to a parent like this? The first step is to realize that your old parent-child dynamic isn't working anymore. If you act submissive or defensive, your parent will keep calling the shots. And realize, too, that doing the opposite—deciding, "I need to be the parent now"—won't work either. It'll simply make your parent dig in even harder (just like you did as a kid).

Instead, try something different: Put on your salesperson's hat and pull out a classic sales trick called the *assumptive close*.

In the business world, if you're meeting with a client who's considering buying new office chairs, you don't close your meeting by saying, "So, are you interested in buying the chairs?" Instead, you say, "Would you like us to deliver the chairs this week or next week?" In short, you assume that the sale is a done deal.

Now, here's how to use this approach with an aging parent who can no longer be independent. Instead of arguing over this fact—"Dad, you know this isn't working out"—simply act as if the decision is already made. In a friendly, matter-of-fact tone, say something like, "It's getting to that time when you need people to help you. So I'm wondering—do you want an upscale living facility like Aunt Rosie chose, or do you think you'd be more comfortable in a homier setting?"

Or say, "Since driving isn't a good option for you right now, what do you think would work better for you—a car service or a taxi? And would you rather sell the car or give it to one of the grandkids?"

When you do this, don't feel like you're engaging in trickery. Instead, realize that you're doing this out of love and a desire to protect your aging parent. This will help you stay firm and follow through.

And don't get sucked into being explanatory. ("Really, Mom, it's for the best, because you keep falling and you can't even cook for yourself.") Instead, be declaratory: "It's time. Let's work out the details together."

Remember: The deal is done. And when you truly believe this yourself, there's a pretty good chance you'll convince your parent as well.

A Bonus Trick

Another effective approach for dealing with irrational parents is to force them out of their heads and into their lives. Here's how:

If your parent starts complaining—for instance, saying, "Everyone thinks I'm worthless," or, "My life stinks"—don't go down that rabbit hole. Instead, simply say something like, "I understand how you feel. Now, what's for lunch?"

The more you do this, the more you keep your parent moving forward instead of wallowing in complaints and grievances. This approach is especially effective with parents who are suffering from mild dementia, but it'll work with the ones who are mentally sharp as well.

Usable insight ••••••••••••••••••••••••

Give a person a choice between A or B, and you'll often distract them from rejecting both.

Action Steps

1. If your aging parent is resisting getting help, determine the type of assistance that's required—for instance, assisted living, a home health aide, or a car service. Then check out the local resources to learn about what's available.

2. Craft and practice your assumptive close so you can deliver it calmly and assertively.

3. Once you make your assumptive close, stick with it. Do not allow yourself to get sucked into discussions about why the person doesn't need or want help.

•••

chapter 29

The Four *H*'s and Four *R*'s

Rebuilding a Personal Relationship
After an Irrational Person Breaks It

SOMETIMES irrational people will momentarily upset or annoy you. When this happens, it's pretty easy for you to get past it.

Sometimes, however, these people wound you deeply. And that's especially true when they're the people closest to you: your parents, children, or life partners. In this case, you can wind up broken. Something that was whole within you—your trust, your self-esteem, your reputation, your spirit—has been damaged by the person's actions. As a result, you may be consumed by anger. And I understand that, totally. I've been there myself.

But here's the thing: This anger hurts you a lot more than it hurts the other person. One thing I know from decades of counseling people who've been hurt is that holding on to a grudge keeps a victim stuck. And letting go can set that victim free.

If you're holding a grudge against a person who's hurt you deeply—not someone who's truly evil, but someone who treated you badly because he was irrational—it's time to get past it. And there's a good way to do it. I call this strategy the Four *H*'s and Four *R*'s. In addition to helping you heal, this strategy will tell you clearly whether your relationship with the person is salvageable.

The Four *H*'s

To begin your healing, you first need to recognize that the person's actions damaged you deeply in four ways:

Hurt: First, the person hurt you. You experienced intense, devastating pain. And this pain wasn't just emotional; it was also spiritual and even physical. (That's why people often say that a betrayal was "a blow to my gut.")

Hate: Second, the person caused you to hate her. That direct blow to your gut, mind, and soul ripped a hole in you, and it enraged you. While you once saw this person as an ally, or maybe as someone neutral, you now see her as your enemy.

Hesitant to Trust: Third, the person made you hesitant to trust her again. When someone wounds you, it makes you afraid that it will happen again, and that if it does, you may not survive it.

Hold a Grudge: Finally, the person caused you to hold on to a grudge, which you're doing largely to protect yourself because it lets you keep your guard up. And that grudge makes you a lesser person than you want to be.

The Four *R*'s

Once you identify all the ways in which the person hurt you, it's time to switch from the Four *H*'s to the Four *R*'s. These are what you require from the other person in order for you to forgive.

If the person is still trapped in crazy, it's not yet time to implement the Four *R*'s. But if you believe that the person is sincerely interested in healing your relationship and is sane enough to try, schedule a time when you and the person can be alone and are both feeling calm. Then say something like, "When _____ happened, you didn't just disappoint me. You broke something in me. Right now, I want you to look me in the eyes so I can show you how much you hurt me. Because if you don't see it, I'll have trouble believing that you won't do it again."

State emphatically, "I'm not doing this to punish you or make you feel guilty. I'm doing it because I need to believe you." Then describe how the person hurt you—emotionally, spiritually, and physically. Stay calm but don't hold back.

Next, describe the feelings of hate you experienced as a result of that hurt. Again, stay calm but don't sugarcoat anything, even if you see the person flinching or crying. After that, tell the person how her acts left you feeling so wounded and betrayed that you're hesitant to trust her, or possibly to trust anyone.

Finally, say, "Because of what you did, I am holding a grudge against you. I don't like holding a grudge, and I want to let it go."

At this point, if there is any hope for your relationship, the person will still be listening to you. If so, it's time to move on to the Four R's. Tell the person, "There are four things I need from you." Then talk through each one:

Remorse: Say, "The first thing I need is to believe that you feel remorse for what you did. That is the only thing that will let me feel that you haven't just blown the incident off." Be very clear here: You're not asking for regret. Regret is saying, "Okay, I messed up. I'm sorry. It won't happen again, I promise. Can we just move on?" Regret is almost insulting. It's like a dishonest politician saying, "Mistakes were made." But if the person experiences remorse, she will feel incredible and almost unbearable pain for having hurt you. So if you look in her eyes and see real pain, that's the first *R*.

Restitution: Remorse isn't enough, so it's time to move on to the second *R*, restitution. Say, "When I suffered this hurt, you broke something in me. And to fix that, I need some form of payback." If the person hurt you financially, that payback may be money. If the person hurt you emotionally, then say, "This is what I want you to do. I am going to vent about what you did to me and how it hurt me. And I want you to listen without trying to argue or defend yourself until I'm completely done." Then vent. And don't stop until you've drained all the poison from your wound.

Rehabilitation: At this point, it's time for the third *R*. Rehabilitation is where you need to see that the person has learned to deal with issues in a better, saner way. Say something like, "In order to forgive you, I need to know that in the future, you're going to deal with upsets, disappointments, and frustrations in a way other than abusing me. Going forward, I need to see a track record. Furthermore, I need to see that you actually enjoy dealing with things in a healthy way, because if you're only doing this for me, then you're not truly rehabilitated. And if I believe that, I'm going to continue to hesitate to trust you or let you back into my life, just in case you do it again." Next say, "I need to see that over the next six months, you will make the first three *R*'s—remorse, restitution, and rehabilitation—part of your personality." If the person agrees, stand by your part of the agreement. Give her six months to put new, sane behaviors into practice and make them habit.

Requesting forgiveness: At the end of this time, if the person is committed to behaving in a healthy way, say, "I am willing to forgive you completely and let go of my grudge if you are willing to request my forgiveness." If you receive a genuine apology in this moment— one that you can tell comes from the person's heart—then it's your turn. Say, "I forgive you completely in return. And I appreciate the work you did to regain my trust."

At every social gathering, Kaylin's husband, Ed, was the life of the party—until he got drunk. Then he'd humiliate her by getting loud, arguing with other guests, telling off-color jokes, and sometimes nearly passing out.

Before Kaylin's sister got married, Kaylin made Ed promise to keep his drinking under control at the wedding reception. But every time she looked at him, he had another scotch in his hand. Two hours into the reception, he was smashed. An hour later, he made a crude remark to the bride, and the groom ordered him to leave.

Ed's crazy actions mortified Kaylin in front of her friends and family. Her sister had to edit out some important parts of her reception video because Ed had ruined the moments. And Kaylin wasn't sure she could ever fully repair her relationship with her family.

When I talked with Kaylin, her pain was evident—and so was her anger. She didn't trust Ed, and she could barely even stand to be around him. She told me she didn't think she could ever forgive him.

Eventually, I got her to talk about the qualities that had attracted her to Ed in the first place. He was kind. He was a good provider. He had a great sense of humor. And he never drank too much when he was home.

Kaylin decided to give Ed another chance. That night, she said, "We need to talk." Ed guessed correctly that a sledgehammer was about to come down on his head. But to his credit, he sat and waited.

"First," said Kaylin, "I want you to know how deeply you've hurt me. You embarrassed me in front of the people I love, and you damaged my relationship with my sister. Your actions made me sick to my stomach. Every time I think about what you did, I feel like throwing up. And I need to know that you feel remorse about that."

Ed started to cry. "I know," he said. "I did a horrible thing, and I ruined one of the most important days of your life. I am so sorry. If I could erase it all, I would."

"You can't," said Kaylin. "But here's what you can do. First, you can sit there and take it while I vent about this. Because I have a lot to say."

Ed listened. For an hour, he said nothing while Kaylin vented about every time Ed had ruined an event by drinking too much. Their second anniversary. Their fifth anniversary. Last Thanksgiving.

When she finally ran down, Ed apologized again. "I guess I got in the habit of drinking too much at parties in college," he said. "And I think I do it just because I'm not good at social gatherings and it makes me less nervous. But I need to stop at one drink—or at none. I'm so sorry."

But Kaylin said, "An apology right now isn't good enough. You need to show me that you're never going to do this again. You have to prove to me that you can deal with parties and celebrations without losing control. And you have to show me that you're happy to do this—not just that you're doing it to keep me from being hurt and angry."

Ed agreed. And Kaylin put him to the test by saying yes to every party invitation they got over the next six months. Ed was a perfect gentleman at each event, and he didn't even have one drink.

In addition, Ed took it upon himself to meet with Kaylin's sister and her husband and apologize to them. He also apologized personally to Kaylin's mother, father, and grandmother.

At the end of the six months, Ed came home one day and said, "I have a request."

"What?" Kaylin asked.

"I would like to take you out to dinner," he said. "But before we go, I have something important to ask you. Do you forgive me?"

"Yes," she said.

When Kaylin forgave Ed, she set him free from his guilt. But more important, she set herself free from her grudge. And Ed's commitment to the Four *R*'s told her she could trust him again.

If he'd balked at any of them, she could still have let go of her grudge. And a negative response might have told her that she needed to let go of Ed as well.

When you try this strategy, be willing to accept either outcome: forgiveness or a clean break. As I've said, this is more about you than it is about the other person. If the person does come around, that's gravy. But either way, you'll erase the stain of anger from your own soul, and that's what matters most.

TIP

Here's a thought to keep in mind: If you're the one who has hurt, injured, or betrayed another person, you may be the one who has driven that person crazy. If that's the case, you may need to offer your Four *R*'s to address the Four *H*'s you caused.

Usable insight •

Anger is like swallowing poison and hoping the other person dies.

Action Steps

1. Think hard about your relationships with the irrational people in your life.

2. Identify situations in which you were hurt deeply by these people.

3. Ask yourself honestly if you are holding a grudge. If so, decide that you need to clear this toxin from your own system, no matter what the outcome will be.

• •

SECTION 5

What to Do When Crazy Is Actually Mental Illness

When you're dealing with a loved one who has a severe emotional disorder or a mental illness, you can't talk to crazy all by yourself. In this situation, you'll need serious help from the pros.

But which pros do you need—and how do you get a person to agree to see them? I'll answer both questions in this section, and I'll also talk about how to find out if someone who's in a dark place is at risk for suicide or may be contemplating a terrible act of violence.

chapter 30

Where to Turn When Crazy Is Above Your Pay Grade

THERE'S regular crazy, which you can deal with on your own. That's what most of this book is about. And then there's serious crazy, which I'll cover in this section. That's a whole different story. This kind of irrationality includes:

▶ Mental illnesses like depression, bipolar disorder, severe anxiety, posttraumatic stress disorder (PTSD), or schizophrenia

▶ Severe behavior problems

▶ Personality disorders (discussed in Chapter 4)

▶ Drug or alcohol addiction

▶ Homicidal thinking

▶ Any kind of suicidal thinking or behavior, or any serious self-destructive behavior such as anorexia or cutting

▶ Even garden-variety irrationality—for instance, the behavior of a rebellious teen or hostile employee—when your efforts to handle it on your own don't succeed

▸ Any kind of irrational behavior that continually causes a severe amygdala hijack in you, because that's your brain's way of saying, "This is some serious s#@&"

When you're dealing with issues like these, you need to call for professional help. That's especially true if the person you're dealing with is potentially dangerous. This is not the time to use the do-it-yourself tools I've described in this book.

However, this raises a question: What kind of help should you seek for a person with a mental illness or other serious psychological issue? Recently, I realized that simply telling people to "get help" isn't good enough advice. That's because it's hard for most people to know where to turn when they're at the end of their rope.

It took me a long time to understand that the field we call mental health can be a bewildering place for laypeople to navigate. That's because different issues require different approaches. Sometimes a person needs professional counseling. Sometimes he needs rehab to keep from falling back into mental illness or addiction. And sometimes he needs psychotherapy or psychiatry.

How do you decide? I can't give you a specific answer without knowing what kind of issue you're dealing with, but the following look at different types of mental healthcare can help steer you in the right direction.

Medically Oriented Psychiatry

Medically oriented psychiatry is where to start if the person has a personality disorder (see Chapter 4), another form of mental illness, or a very serious emotional problem. And it's definitely your first stop if the person is suicidal, self-destructive, or in any way a potential or actual danger to others.

To understand the role of a psychiatrist, think of an emergency room doctor who stabilizes a patient after a car accident and then sends the patient off to rehab. Similarly, the role of a psychiatrist is to stabilize a patient's neurobiology, using medications or other medical approaches, so the person can benefit from psychotherapy.

When do you need this level of help? Call a psychiatrist if someone in your life is:

▶ Talking about committing suicide

▶ Suffering from severe PTSD

▶ Committing violent acts

▶ Saying threatening things to you or others

▶ Suffering from depression

▶ Suffering from severe anxiety or panic attacks

▶ Experiencing auditory or visual hallucinations

▶ Exhibiting severe self-injurious behavior like cutting or anorexia

▶ Suffering from a life-threatening addiction

▶ Showing signs of a severe personality disorder

If you do schedule an appointment for the person with a psychiatrist, be realistic about what to expect. Psychiatrists can't cure serious mental or emotional problems with a pill. Often, however, they can bring patients to a higher level of functioning, creating an opportunity for healing.

Here's an example of how a psychiatrist used medication to stabilize a person who was spinning out of control so another professional (typically a psychotherapist—and in this case, me) could lead that person back to sanity.

When Jake turned 18, he went into the U.S. Marines. Sent to Iraq, he was part of a unit that fought in the second battle of Fallujah. His commanding officer ordered him to take out a presumed sniper nest in a crowded area of the city. He followed orders, but when he arrived at the scene, he found that he'd killed an entire family: the parents, two children, a grandfather, and a dog.

Jake was debriefed and followed the recommended procedures for dealing with the psychological impact of causing collateral damage. But the images of that family never went away. When he closed his eyes he saw them even more clearly—especially the dead grandfather, holding one of the dead grandchildren. All the debriefing he received couldn't stop him from believing that he was no longer someone who killed the enemy but instead someone who murdered the innocent.

Jake couldn't sleep, and he had flashbacks and grew deeply depressed. Sometimes he took his gun out of his closet and thought about how easy it would be to end his pain. One day, his girlfriend caught him holding the gun to his head. She persuaded him to put it down and to see a psychiatrist.

Months later, Jake wound up in my office, where two years of psychotherapy helped him see he wasn't a bad man at all. But he had taken his first step toward recovery when the psychiatrist who first saw him convinced him to take an antidepressant. The medication moved him from "I want to die" to "Maybe there's hope"—and that transformation, in turn, allowed him to walk into my office a month later and tell me, "I need help."

Psychotherapy

Psychotherapy was my specialty for many years, and it's where you can turn if the person has a great deal of difficulty coping with life's demands. Psychiatrists, psychologists, and licensed family therapists can provide psychotherapy.

A psychotherapist's job is to help a person learn not to overreact, take things too personally, jump to conclusions, blame others, make excuses, feel chronic self-pity, or live life in the grip of destructive false ideas and limiting beliefs. In other words, the psychotherapist helps people realize that what is, is, and what isn't, isn't—and helps them learn not to treat a small thing like a big thing or treat a big thing like a small thing.

Psychotherapy is hard work. Sometimes it takes years. But when a person is willing to commit to it, it can turn a life around. Here's an example, involving a patient of mine who was molested at age 9 by her 13-year-old brother.

Tessa told me that at first, she hid her molestation from her parents. Her brother was the superstar athlete her mother and father doted on, and she was terrified of how they'd react.

Finally, when she couldn't take it any longer, she spoke up. When she told her parents, however, her fears came true. Her mother and father told her she'd imagined the incident and was simply jealous of her popular brother. They asked her how she could make such an ugly accusation. (The truth came out later, when her brother raped a fellow student in high school.)

When the molestation first occurred, Tessa's immediate thought was, "My brother is touching me where he shouldn't." However, she was terrified by his threats and went along with his demands. But unconsciously, she thought that maybe she was a bad, dirty, sickening person for doing what he wanted. Her parents' harsh response when she told them about her brother's actions just confirmed this thought in her mind.

Tessa felt dirty and disgusting, which led her to act out sexually with boys at school. This earned her a reputation as the class slut. She developed the false belief that she was the cool one who was in control of these boys (in a way that she could never control her brother). In addition, her sexual activity gave her a way to get back at her parents for not believing her. In effect, she was saying, "You want to see how awful I am? I'll show you!"

Tessa believed that she wasn't worth liking or loving or even believing, and that she was only worth using for sex. But she didn't care, because she hated the world. Her belief allowed her to say to everyone, "You can't hurt me, because I don't care—and I'll show you how little I care."

However, things had changed by the time she was in her early 30s when she came to see me. She'd found and married a man who truly loved her and didn't use her. But because of her self-destructive beliefs, she couldn't relax or enjoy sex with him, frustrating both of them.

As Tessa told me her story, she began to realize that she wasn't afraid of her husband using her. Instead, she was terrified of his truly accepting and loving her, because that meant she was safe. And she feared that if she finally felt safe, the pain of a lifetime of not feeling safe would wash her away. Just telling her that she was afraid to feel safe caused her to cry nearly uncontrollably.

During our sessions, I helped Tessa to think of her past wounds as an abscess that she needed to drain. She realized that safety was like a knife that wasn't hurting her but instead allowing her to drain all the pain inside. And when she let that happen, she began healing from the inside out.

Psychosocial Rehabilitation

Psychosocial rehabilitation is an underappreciated, underfunded, and understaffed area of the mental health system—yet it's critical to the stability of people who are battling mental illness or addiction.

Over and over again, I've met with patients, couples, and families who sincerely agreed to do things after they left a hospital, a clinic, or my office and in some cases even signed contracts. I know they meant it. But often, as soon as they were left to their own recognizance, *wham!*—they went right back to the challenges and temptations of real life, and my treatment plan went out the window.

Why? Because all we can do in a clinical setting is stabilize a person's condition. To be truly effective, treatment also needs to happen in the real world.

Luckily, the mental health field is finally recognizing this. Increasingly, federal, state, and local agencies are funding rehab programs that offer long-term, in-home treatment as well as intensive out-patient care. Other programs are giving professionals and families the training they need to help recovering people stay on course.

I'm personally involved with two of these programs. One is the Life Adjustment Team (LAT) in California, whose staff members help patients with everything from shopping to finding a job and paying bills. Another is the LEAP Institute in New York, which teaches professionals and families around the world how to provide long-term help for people coping with serious mental issues.

I've become an evangelist for organizations like these because the financial, emotional, and psychological toll of relapse and recidivism is unacceptable. What really opened my eyes was realizing that the majority of school shootings might have been prevented if the shooters hadn't fallen through the cracks after a prior contact with the mental health profession.

If someone you care about receives treatment for a mental illness or addiction and you want to help protect the person from a relapse, find out what types of rehab programs your community provides. Then reach out for help. With long-term support from the pros and you, the person you care about will have a far greater chance not just of getting well but of staying well.

After seeing the remarkable results that LAT achieves with its clients (it doesn't call them patients), I wanted to find out how it did what it did and why it worked. So I interviewed clients, their families, and the case managers who work at LAT.

One day I interviewed the entire LAT team of 16 case managers about what they thought was their secret sauce. It quickly became clear that this was an unusual group of professionals. They could be working for more money in institutional settings, but they chose LAT because they could spend up to nine hours per week with each client rather than seeing people for an hour or less each week. They also treated clients where they lived, going to their homes or treatment centers. By acting as teachers, mentors, and coaches, they were able to make sure their clients took their medications, made it to their doctors' appointments, and lived as independently as possible. With their clients' permission, they also could alert psychiatrists about acute crises.

LAT's approach is simple: Stability, activity, and productivity are the keys that help their clients get back to life.

I asked one client what helped him. "Here's something most people don't understand," he said. "When you're about to be discharged from a psychiatric facility and you're meeting with the psychiatrist, the social worker, the psychologist, and the nurse, and they give you a list of everything you need to do, you smile politely at them and don't remember anything they said. Even if they write it down, it's overwhelming. What you need is someone to do those things with you. And it can't be your mom or dad, because there's usually too much tension in that relationship."

Another client told me, "When I meet with my case manager, the first thing I see is a huge smile on her face. It's been years since I put that kind of smile on anyone's face, because everyone is so damned serious and so worried about whether I'm following through with everything I'm supposed to be doing. I'll tell you, when someone is glad to see you for who you are as a human being and is totally accepting of you, you're much more likely to open up and talk with them about your problems."

Counseling

Counseling and psychotherapy overlap, but in general, counseling is less intense. (Think of it as therapy lite.) Typically, a counselor assesses a person's problems in dealing effectively with life, work, and relationships, and proposes solutions.

Counseling can help a person with a mental illness work through life issues once that person no longer needs intensive therapy. And counseling is a strong choice when you're not dealing with real mental illness but instead are finding garden-variety crazy impossible to handle on your own.

For example, a counselor can help you if you want to make a marriage stronger, if you need help dealing with a disruptive child, or if you want advice for dealing with a difficult parent. And in the business world, a counselor can help you deal with irrational clients or coworkers who don't respond to your own attempts to talk to crazy. Here's an example.

As a business consultant, I wear many hats, and one of them is coach or counselor. In this role, I spend a lot of my time negotiating cease-fires in office wars.

A while ago, I counseled two employees at a real estate firm, Jack and Shelley. Jack, a senior manager, both mentored and tormented Shelley, his rising star. He would talk loudly, make obnoxious comments, and embarrass Shelley when they met with clients. But he was an incredibly smart top producer whose clients liked him because he always came up with the best deals for them.

Shelley had learned a lot from Jack, but now she was becoming confident in her own abilities. And she was reaching the point where she couldn't stand listening to Jack's comments, which she said felt like "nails on a chalkboard" to her.

Jack didn't want to break up their partnership because he was fond of Shelley and liked having her as his partner. In addition, he enjoyed watching her grow professionally.

Shelley finally brought Jack into my office, where I met with them together. I liked Shelley, and I liked Jack, too. Maybe that's because I always knew where he was coming from. I found him refreshing compared to the passive-aggressive people I often deal with.

When I was pretty sure I'd established a rapport with Jack, I said out loud what I believed Shelley felt but couldn't say: "Jack creeps me out and makes my skin crawl." Surprisingly, this didn't seem to upset Jack. But getting it out in the open caused Shelley to start crying almost uncontrollably and with great relief.

I told Jack it was clear that Shelley wanted me to smooth out some of his "repulsive" qualities. Sensing that I liked him and enjoyed talking with him, Jack agreed with very little hesitation.

In my first individual session with Jack, I asked him why he'd agreed to see me, especially after what I'd said about Shelley's feelings in the prior session. He told me, "Look, I knew she felt that way. And I also know that some aspects of my personality work against me and that even I'm sick of them."

Jack's words didn't surprise me. Shelley wasn't able to see his desire to become less obnoxious, but I'd guessed at it in our first session. I told Jack he was so smart that he owed it to himself not to do anything that distracted people from his abilities, and he agreed.

Finally, before he left that day, I told him, "I know a secret that nobody else in the world knows about you. It's possible that even you don't know it. Would you like to know what it is?"

He smiled and said, "Sure," as if knowing he was about to receive one of my obnoxious comments.

I smiled back. "The secret I know about you," I said, "is that deep down you're not an a--hole. But rest assured, your secret is safe with me."

He laughed and replied, "I'm looking forward to seeing what you can do with me. How far do you think you can get with me?"

"It may be that the best you can be is an A-I-R," I playfully replied.

"What's an A-I-R?" Jack asked.

"That's an a--hole in recovery," I said. "But you need to keep at it, because it's an addiction."

He laughed. "I guess that seals the deal!"

"Maybe it takes one to know one," I bantered back.

Still needing to have the last word, Jack replied a little more seriously, "Maybe it takes one to help one."

Mentoring and Support Groups

Do you have someone in your life who makes you a better person? Who sees your special gifts and strengths, and offers guidance to help you reach your potential? Who won't put up with your self-defeating, counterproductive behaviors?

Well, guess what. People with mental illnesses or other serious mental or emotional problems need mentors, too. In fact, they need them even more than you do.

These people face huge life issues. They battle crippling medication side effects, financial problems, loneliness, and often addictions. Their own thoughts and feelings often terrify them. Other people stigmatize and marginalize them.

Under the circumstances, it's easy for these people to give up. To say, "I'm not taking the drug that makes me nauseated." "I'm not going into work." "I'm not getting out of bed." "I'm just going to have one drink." "I don't have any reason to go on."

This is where mentors can save lives by offering support, love, advice, and sometimes a swift kick in the butt. If you're fortunate enough to live near a program like LAT, mentoring is part of the package. If not, look around you. Who else genuinely cares for the person you're trying to help? For instance, would a caring priest, rabbi, or teacher be willing to accept a mentoring role?

Also, harness the power of support groups. While the people in these groups aren't professionals, they have their own kind of expertise. In fact, some of the most powerful mentoring is done by other people who are going through the same hell—or have found their way out of it. From Alcoholics Anonymous to the National Alliance on Mental Illness, there are organizations that can help. A therapist can steer you to the right group for the person in your life.

While you're at it, find people or groups who can mentor and support *you* as you support a person who's battling mental illness, addiction, or any other problem that causes serious irrationality. These groups can help you with practical issues—for instance, how to obtain housing for an adult child or how to protect yourself if a spouse gets violent. And just as important, they can help you come to terms with your own feelings of grief, anger, guilt, or loneliness. They can laugh with you and cry with you. They can give you the strength to keep going when you think you can't. And they can allow you to talk openly about things that might horrify "civilians" who aren't fighting the same battles that you are.

Wendy, a friend of mine, has a daughter with autism. Doctors diagnosed Wendy's daughter years ago, back when autism was almost unheard of. Wendy didn't know anyone else with an autistic child, and she felt completely alone.

"I remember one day in particular," Wendy told me. "I took my daughter to a doctor's appointment and was driving her back to school. She thought that she was going home to play, and when she saw that we were heading to school instead, she started smashing her head over and over again against the car window and screaming hysterically. Here we were, in the center lane on a major San Diego freeway, and I looked over and saw blood gushing from her nose and running down the car window as she kept screaming and hitting the window. And I thought, 'Someone in a passing car is going to see this screaming, bloody child and call the police.'"

Somehow, Wendy got her daughter to school and cleaned up her bloody nose. When she got back home, she was still shaking. "It was one of the scariest experiences I can remember," she said. She told her friends about the episode, and they were sympathetic. But they didn't really understand, and Wendy could see that talking about it made them uncomfortable.

A few weeks later, Wendy found a support group for parents of children with autism. Not knowing what to expect, she attended a meeting in the living room of one of the parents. After the other parents said hello, they asked her, "How's it going?"

"I told them about the freeway drive," she said. And they not only understood, they shared their own horror stories for the week.

One dad talked about how his son came home from a social skills training course and immediately told a close family friend, "My teacher says never to tell you that you're really fat." A mom talked about how terrified she was when her son escaped from home over the weekend. (He turned up in the swimming pool at a nearby church facility, bewildering a group of nuns.) A third said the Border Patrol had nearly arrested her adult son because he couldn't tell them who he was.

As she heard one story after another, Wendy realized that everyone in the room was dealing with the same kind of crazy she was enduring. "And another thing I discovered," she said, "is that we spent as much time laughing as we did being upset. Somehow, just sharing the crazy stuff we had to deal with every day made us see the humor in it."

In fact, Wendy says, the next week, when her daughter knocked a hole in a hospital wall while waiting for an MRI, she initially freaked out—and then she thought, "Ha. Let's see if anybody can top this story at the next meeting."

Finding the Right Fit

In this chapter, I hope I've offered some insight into the kinds of help you can find if you're dealing with someone who's struggling with a mental illness or any other serious form of crazy. But no matter which route you choose, be aware that it may take more than one try to find the right doctor, therapist, rehab agency, mentor, or support group.

For instance, I've had patients come to me after seeing two or three other therapists, none of whom did anything wrong, but for some reason the chemistry wasn't right. And I'm guessing that more than once, a patient left me for another therapist who turned out to be a better fit.

So if the person you're trying to aid agrees to seek help, persist until you find the right provider. Also, realize that you will probably need not just one person but a team, which may include a psychiatrist, a therapist or counselor, a rehab program, and a support group of people who can mentor and encourage both of you. Fighting serious crazy is a tough battle, and the more reinforcements you can line up, the better.

Usable insight ••••••••••••••••••••••••

The key to fixing a big problem is to select the right tools.

Action Steps

1. If the person you're trying to help is currently dangerous or may be suicidal, call a trusted family doctor and get a referral to a medically oriented psychiatrist immediately.

2. If you feel that you have some time, do a little research. Begin by contacting organizations that focus on the specific problem you're dealing with (such as borderline personality disorder, PTSD, or depression). These organizations can offer advice about the best resources in your area. If you're dealing with garden-variety crazy that you can't handle on your own, interview several counselors or psychotherapists and select the one you like best.

3. Find a support group that can help the person you're involved with handle the challenges of life. Then find a support group to help you cope.

••• ▬▬▬▬▬▬

chapter 31

How to Get the Person to Say Yes to Getting Help

IT'S ONE THING to decide that someone who's battling serious mental issues needs to seek help, and it's another to get that person to agree to seek help. This is a tough job—as you already know if you've tried it. And that's why I'm devoting an entire chapter to it.

Why is it so hard to get a person who's mentally ill to agree to undergo treatment? Because in this situation, you're not just dealing with denial or defensiveness. Instead, there's a good chance you're dealing with a phenomenon called *anosognosia*, in which mentally ill people don't believe they're mentally ill. It isn't that they're too stubborn or scared to admit the truth. Instead, the fact that they have an illness simply isn't real to them.

My friend Xavier Amador, who heads the LEAP Institute I mentioned in Chapter 30, stresses the need to understand that anosognosia is actually a symptom of mental illness, just like hallucinations or paranoia. You can't change it by talking a person out of it any more than you can talk a person with paranoid schizophrenia out of hearing voices or thinking that the FBI is out to get him.

Breaking through the anosognosia of a person with mental illness is very tough. In fact, it's so difficult that I recommend you approach it using the same steps I teach hostage negotiators.

Here is the five-step process. (It's important to remember that in the first three steps, you are not trying to convince the person to seek help. That happens in steps 4 and 5, after you've created a new dynamic between the two of you.)

1. Listen

The first step in reaching a noncooperative person, whether it's a mentally ill family member or a homicidal hostage taker, is to stop talking and start listening.

I know it's hard to listen deeply and calmly to a person who's extremely irrational. Your natural impulse is to counter the person's crazy talk with logic, to plead with the person, or even to yell or cry. But as I explained in Chapters 1 and 2, that doesn't work even with garden-variety crazy. And it's dangerously wrong when you're facing down severe irrationality.

Here's what I want you to do instead: Find a quiet time every few days when you can sit down with the person. Then gently and empathetically encourage the person to talk about what's going on inside. Here are some questions you can ask:

- "How do you feel right now? How are you sleeping? Are you eating okay?"
- "What scares you the most right now?"
- "What frustrates you right now?"
- "What makes you sad?"
- "What would make you happier?"
- "What are your goals?"
- "What are your dreams?"
- "How is work going for you right now?"
- "How is school going for you right now?"

Also ask, "What's the worst thing for you right now?" (which I discussed in Chapter 26).

When you ask these questions, you may get some crazy answers. For instance, a person with bipolar disorder might say, "My goal is to win an Oscar next year"—even if she's not an actor. Or a person who's paranoid might say, "What scares me the most is that you're out to get me."

I don't care. No matter what the person says, don't disagree. Don't say, "That's unrealistic." Don't say, "I'm not out to get you."

Just listen. And then use conversation deepeners such as:

‣ "Say more about that."

‣ "What's it like for you to think that I'm out to get you?"

‣ "Yes, I see."

‣ "Hmmm."

‣ "Okay."

‣ "Really?"

‣ "What else scares you right now?"

Also, paraphrase some important things the person says, to show that you're listening deeply. For example, if she says, "I'm scared that I'll never be able to get a job again," say, "That's really tough to feel afraid that you won't be able to work again."

Finally, help the person label her feelings. Remember that the simple act of labeling an emotion helps a person calm down. For example, say, "I can see that talking about this makes you feel very sad," or, "It's hard to talk about this, and I can see that it makes you feel angry."

Above all, do not make suggestions. Don't try to fix any issues the person describes. Don't picture the person as a problem you need to solve.

Just listen.

One challenge in listening like this is to do it without agreeing with the person's crazy ideas. Here are two tricks that hostage negotiators use:

> ▶ Apologize for disagreeing. For instance, in a hostage situation, a negotiator might say, "I'm sorry we can't get a helicopter here for you." Similarly, you can tell an adult child who's suffering from depression, "I'm sorry it upsets you when we talk about why we think medication might help you."

> ▶ Be humble. For instance, say, "I know the situation looks very different to you. While I think medication would make you feel much better, I could be wrong."

It will take serious self-control to listen without inserting your own ideas, especially if the other person is saying wildly crazy things. But when you listen to the person without an agenda, you'll begin to build an entirely different relationship. And that's the first step toward a breakthrough.

When I first met Alice, who suffered from delusional depression, she strongly resisted the idea of getting any treatment at all. I wasn't sure why, and I needed to find out. So I just kept listening, and eventually, she said something that gave me a clue.

"Every day," she said, "I'm afraid that someone is going to come and force me to go into a psychiatric hospital."

Paraphrasing her words, I said, "So you're afraid every day that someone is going to come and force you to go into a psychiatric hospital. Is that what you're saying?" (It might seem like repeating people's words in this way is belittling, but people rarely feel that way. Instead, they nearly always feel acknowledged.)

"Yes," Alice replied.

"Say more about that," I encouraged her.

"Five years ago, my parents called the police," she said. "They took me to a psychiatric hospital and even restrained my arms and legs. I still remember it every day."

To encourage her to say more, I asked, "Really?"

"Oh, it was awful," she added, with even more emotion. "I don't know how I survived."

"How awful did it get at its worst?" I asked.

"I was terrified that someone was going to kill me," she said.

When Alice told me her story, I knew why she was reluctant to get professional help. Clearly, she saw every professional—including me—as someone who might drag her back to a mental hospital and put her life in danger. Knowing that I was going to have to work hard to turn myself from a threat into an ally, I moved on to step 2.

The Bio-Psycho-Social Approach to Listening

Like many mental health professionals, I view mental illness as having biopsychosocial components. *Bio* refers to the biology of mental illness, as in possible neurochemical imbalances that are often best treated with medication. *Psycho* refers to the psychology of mental illness, as in how the patient psychologically copes with frustration, upsets, and disappointment. *Social* obviously refers to social factors, as in the possible loss of a relationship or a job or feeling ostracized by a group.

To me, listening to mental illness involves first asking the person about physical symptoms such as sleep, appetite, pains, or sexual functioning, to uncover what's going on biologically. Next, it involves asking what has frustrated, disappointed, scared, or angered the person and what the person has done or is doing to deal with the situation. And finally, it involves asking the person to talk about relationships with intimate others, family, friends, and job or school situations.

2. Empathize

To break through to someone, you need to feel what that person is feeling. This is hard when you're dealing with someone whose feelings make no sense to you, whether it's a ranting hostage holder or a mentally ill person who's frightened because she's seeing snakes coming out of the walls.

But hard or not, it's necessary, and when you succeed, the payoff can be huge.

For example, Sue, a patient of mine, told me that she hadn't dated in more than two decades. Only a few minutes later, she said, "The men I'm dating are always thinking about raping me. I constantly have to be on my guard."

Now, I could have said, "If you aren't dating at all, you can't be dating men who think about raping you."

But what would that accomplish? Basically, I'd just reinforce what everyone else in her life told her: You're crazy. And she didn't need to hear that again.

Instead, I paused. And I imagined myself feeling what she felt. And then I said, "I'm sorry. You must feel very lonely."

Immediately, I saw tears well up in Sue's eyes. Not tears of sadness—tears because finally, someone got how she felt.

When you show a mentally ill person true empathy in this way, something magical will happen. That's because when you mirror the person's thoughts and feelings, the person starts to mirror *your* thoughts and feelings.

When Alice told me about her mental hospital experience, I responded, "It must be awful to carry around the memory of being taken away by the police, being forced to go into a psychiatric hospital, and thinking someone was going to kill you. And it must be awful not knowing how you survived and worrying that it could happen again."

Alice, who'd already been tearful, now sobbed openly with relief that I'd heard her out and didn't judge her or minimize her feelings.

When I spoke with Alice in this way, I completely mirrored her feeling of distress. In return, she began to mirror my feelings when I expressed them. And as a result, she became ever so slightly more willing to consider my opinions and advice.

When you empathize with a mentally ill person, it makes the person less defensive and less resistant to listening to you. And, treatment issues aside, it makes her feel less alone and more like a human being who matters. Regardless of where you end up, you'll both be in a better place than where you started out.

Say "Hello in There"

A while ago, I had a vivid, terrifying dream. It was one of those rare dreams that seemed so real that even after I woke up, I felt like what happened was real.

In my dream, I was a homeless, schizophrenic man. A group of people were asking me to do simple things—things that were simple to them—and they got angry when I couldn't. And I just kept pushing them back and pushing them back. Desperately, I thought, "You think it's simple, but I can't do it!" And there was a point at which I found something like a nail file and I stabbed someone. It was just horrendous.

In the dream, I ran away and hid. I didn't want anyone to see me. I didn't want anyone else to ask me to do simple things I couldn't do. And I didn't want to see people's blank or hostile faces.

When I woke up, I felt that I'd experienced what it's like to be schizophrenic. It was similar to what I've felt many times when I've treated mentally ill or suicidal people and have, at least briefly, entered the "dark night of the soul" where they're trapped.

And as I thought about the dream, I remembered the lyrics from a haunting song by John Prine, "Hello in There." In the song, he pleads with listeners to acknowledge the "invisible" people in society, rather than simply walking past them as if they don't matter.

This is what the mentally ill people in our lives need us to do more than anything. They need us to realize that they're human beings, not just problems or nuisances. They need us to recognize that they're hurting and scared, and that they have worth and deserve respect.

They need us to say, "Hello in there." And that's what listening and empathizing are all about.

3. Agree

When you're dealing with someone who's resisting you, agreeing with that person about anything can set off a positive chain reaction. I call this the *cascade of yes*.

In a hostage situation, for instance, a negotiator might say, "I agree—you've had a really hard life." Or, "I agree that we need to get some food in there for you." If the negotiator is lucky, simple statements like these may eventually build into a cascade of yes that leads the hostage taker to agree to let in a paramedic or release a hostage.

Setting off a cascade of yes is your next step, too. But right now, you're in a tricky position. As I've noted, you can't agree with the crazy things the person believes. Instead, you need to find things you can agree on. Here are some examples:

- If the person says, "I hate my doctor," you can say, "I agree that if my doctor said things that upset me, I wouldn't like her much either."

- If the person says, "I don't want to go to my support group meeting," you can say something like, "Yeah, I totally get that. What a pain to have to leave the house tonight, especially since it's raining. I'll tell you what—when you get home from the meeting, let's do something fun to make up for it."

The key is simply to find common ground, large or small, as often as you can. When you do this consistently, the person will grow less suspicious of you and start seeing you as an ally.

When Alice told me that she didn't want treatment for her symptoms, I couldn't ethically agree with that choice. So I agreed with her feelings.

"You know," I said, "I agree that you went through a terrible experience earlier. And if your experience at the hospital happened to me, and it terrified me—which I think it would—I think I'd have similar fears about getting treatment."

Alice smiled with relief when I agreed with her. So I decided to see if my agreement could start a cascade of yes.

"You know," I continued, "if I had to live every day with the disturbing thoughts and feelings you're having, I'd be interested in exploring ways to make them go away, or at least make them less powerful, even if that meant looking into treatment. What do you think?"

Alice didn't say no. Instead, she said, "Are you thinking of putting me on medications? I can't stand those drugs with all their terrible side effects."

"I think you're ahead of me, Alice," I said. "I'm still imagining what it would feel like to think what you're thinking. And I'm thinking that if I were you, I'd like the thoughts to go away or become less overwhelming, especially if we can find better treatments with fewer side effects, which I agree is crucial. Do you agree with that notion?"

"Yes," Alice replied. "I would like to do something."

Basically, by agreeing with Alice, I'd made her more willing to agree with me. Now I just needed to know what kind of help she needed. To figure that out, I moved to the next step.

4. Understand

As the relationship between you and the person you're trying to help gets stronger, it's time to start talking, cautiously, about treatment. (In a hostage negotiation, this is where you'd start talking about resolving the standoff.)

At this point, you've already gotten to know the person better. Now, however, it's time to dig even deeper. The first step in this process is to learn everything you can about the person's previous experiences (if any) with treatment. To find out what did and didn't work in the past, ask questions such as:

- "How did the medications you took before affect you?"

- "Do you feel that the therapist you saw earlier helped you?"

- "Of all the treatments you've had, what worked best? What didn't work? What made things worse?"

Next, find out what living with the illness is like now by asking:

- "How upsetting are your symptoms right now?"

- "How do they affect your life right now?"

- "What are they costing you?"

- "What would it be like to not have to deal with those symptoms?"

- "How much do you want them to go away?"

If you're lucky, these questions will deepen the person's self-awareness, and she will start actively thinking, "Maybe something really is wrong with me. Maybe I do want to feel better. And maybe there is a way to fix this." And at the same time, the answers will give you more clarity about the steps you need to take next.

I told Alice, "Let's find out everything we can about your thoughts. Tell me if something triggers them or if they come out of nowhere. Tell me how long they last, what you've tried to make them go away, what medications and treatments your other doctors prescribed, and what the results were."

As Alice talked, I took notes. And by the time she was done, I had some ideas about what she needed.

But rather than telling her my thoughts, I said, "This is too important for me to just throw some ideas at you. Instead, I'd like for us to think about everything we've talked about and see what we both think is the best approach. That may include some medications you haven't tried that don't have the side effects of the other ones.

"In the meantime," I added, "think about how important it is to you to stop your negative thoughts or get better control over them. And think about how much it's costing you in terms of your happiness to have to live with those thoughts every day.

"Let's plan to see each other in a week," I concluded. "Then I can tell you what I've come up with and you can tell me how much you want the thoughts to go away or become less intense."

Why didn't I suggest a medication right away? Because patients often resist—and rightly—when a doctor merely writes a prescription without making any effort to understand them. I knew that both Alice and I needed time to process what she'd said and think about what she should do.

By the way, a fellow psychiatrist once told me that 50 percent of patients never return after a first visit to a psychiatrist. I'd rather pay attention up front than condemn my patients to a lousy life because I was too busy to get to know them.

When you take time to understand the mentally ill person in your own life, instead of just saying, "You need a drug," or, "You need therapy," that person won't feel pressured or steamrolled. Instead, she will begin to understand that you're truly trying to help.

And when that happens, you'll be ready for your fifth and final step.

5. Act

If you're lucky, there will now be a new dynamic between you and the person you want to help. And that means you're ready to become allies and work toward finding a solution.

In a hostage situation, this is where you'll get a hostage taker to put down his weapon and surrender. In your case, however, the person will willingly surrender in a different way—by giving up his resistance and agreeing to team up with you to find help.

This doesn't mean, however, that you're now in charge. And it doesn't mean that you can dictate the person's choices when it comes to treatment. Try to do that, and you'll instantly move back to square one.

Instead, realize that the two of you are entering this phase as equal partners. I know that you're the sane one in this relationship, but remember: The other person has more control over what's going to happen next than you do. You can't make decisions unilaterally. You have to make them together. Here's how it worked out for Alice and me.

> Alice came back a week later, saying she was committed to trying a treatment. I described the different options, including medications. I also talked about nonmedication treatments such as cognitive behavioral therapy.
>
> My clinical opinion was that in Alice's case, medication would be more effective than such therapy. But she strongly wanted to try the therapy first, so we did.
>
> As I expected, cognitive behavioral therapy helped a little but not enough. Yet the fact that I hadn't rushed Alice into taking a medication led her to trust me and helped her to accept a referral to a psychopharmacologist I work with. He put her on a new medication, and within six weeks, she was largely symptom-free.

Keeping Your Expectations Real

In this chapter, I've outlined the five steps that will give you your best shot at getting a person with serious mental or emotional problems to agree to seek help. But if I've made this five-step process sound easy and straightforward, I apologize, because most of the time, it isn't.

I was fortunate with Alice because she wasn't as trapped in anosognosia as many mentally ill people are. (Besides, I've had a lot of practice at this.) Once we started, it didn't take long for me to move through these steps.

In your case, however, things may not happen this fast. In fact, they probably won't. People who are mentally ill need time to see that they have a problem and even more time to agree that they need help.

And that's okay. Don't get discouraged, don't argue, and don't get angry.

Instead, just keep listening, empathizing, agreeing, and understanding. And someday, if you're lucky, the person will say, "Yes, I want to get well."

And then, if you're even luckier, the person will say, "Please help me."

Usable insight ••••••••••••••••••••••••••

What you tell a person is less important than what you enable the person to tell you.

Action Steps

1. Listen. Empathize. Agree. Understand.

2. If it doesn't work, regroup and try again.

3. If and when the person is ready to take the fifth step of taking action, work together with the person to find the right treatment approach.

•••••••••••••••••••••••••••••••••

chapter 32

What to Do If You
Think Someone
May Be Suicidal

IF SOMEONE in your life is mentally ill or has serious emotional problems, you need to reach out for professional help, especially if you know or suspect that the person may hurt himself or others.

But sometimes, you can't tell if a person is seriously ill. And that's particularly true when someone is suicidal.

Unfortunately, suicidal people don't always wear a neon sign saying, "I want to kill myself." In fact, most suicidal people won't tell you how they feel. These people aren't suffering from anosognosia, or unawareness of illness, which I discussed in Chapter 31. Instead, they're coping with emotions that are too enormous and too terrifying to talk about. And if their emotional torment becomes unbearable, these people will eventually slit their wrists, swallow a bottle of painkillers, hang themselves, or put a gun in their mouth.

Sometimes people reach out for help before they take this final step, but often they don't. For the relatives of many desperate people, the first clue that something is desperately wrong is the suicide note left behind.

Over the years, I've worked with many relatives of people who committed suicide. These people never fully get over it. Even when they're able to move on, the pain is always just below the surface.

I don't want this to happen to you. So if you're living with someone who's in a dark place right now, and you think there's even a
remote chance she may be suicidal, here's my message: You're the
one who needs to reach out. And you need to do it now.

One good way to do this is to ask, "What's the worst thing for
you right now?" (See Chapter 26.) The answer you get may scare
you, but it will also tell you what you need to do next. If you're brave
enough, ask that question today. And if the person you're talking
with expresses any suicidal thoughts, take action immediately.

However . . .

I know that the idea of discussing dark and possibly suicidal feelings with a child, a parent, a partner, or a friend can be utterly terrifying. And I know that with every fiber of your being, you don't
want to have this talk. In fact, you may not be able to bring yourself
to do it.

If you can't scrape up the courage to have this talk, don't. At least,
not at first. Instead, bring up the issue without talking about it.

Start by searching the Internet or your public library for stories,
books, or blog posts written by people who are in the same dark
place as your loved one, for similar reasons. If your loved one is ill,
find articles by other people suffering from the same illness. If your
loved one is unemployed, or exhausted by the strain of coping with
a spouse with Alzheimer's disease, or experiencing PTSD, or going
through a terrible divorce, find articles by people who are in the
same situation.

And I'm not talking about articles that say things like, "Life is full
of challenges, and I know I will grow as a result of this one." Articles
like these often help people who are climbing out of a hole or trying
not to fall into one. But they won't help people who are at the very
bottom of the hole.

Instead, look for articles that reflect the writers' despair, anger,
or hopelessness. Then narrow your choices down to the one that's
the most gut wrenching.

For example, I once wrote an article that included this letter from
Jack, a suicidal teen, to his dad:

Given all the things I'm doing that have disappointed you, I'm hoping you won't just see this as another excuse or a way of manipulating you.

In fact I've been so good at doing both of those, I'm afraid to tell you what I'm about to do and have you think I'm just being dramatic and only trying to get attention or get out of taking responsibility for my actions.

Today, I have a bigger fish to fry.

I'm losing it. I'm losing my mind, my sense of who I am, of where I belong, and I'm spending more and more time wondering if life is worth living.

I know I don't have any reason to feel like ending it. I know that so many people have it worse than me. I even know that I have lots of reasons to live. I just don't feel any of them.

I have felt alone for some time now. It hasn't been a few days or even a few weeks. It's been at least months.

Also, the intensity of rage that I feel not only chills you—which I know is why you back off when it gets really ugly between us—it chills me.

I hate hating you more than I hate you. When I hate you at the level I'm capable of hating you I feel like destroying things. That has escalated and finally shifted to thinking of just destroying me.

But in reality, I don't want to destroy anything, I just want to destroy the pain I feel and make it go away. But it won't go away and I can't make it.

The reason I drink, do drugs, and cut on myself—all of which scare the s#@& out of you—is because they all relieve me. When I'm stone-cold sober and drug-free and the pain and the craziness intensify, all I can think about is numbing myself. I don't do alcohol and drugs to get high, I do them to get by. And when I cut on myself, which terrorizes you, I feel like I'm cutting out the pain or at the very least that I'm feeling something. And that gives me relief from the pain of feeling nothing.

Assuming you won't rub my face in this—and I don't think you want to play Russian roulette with me—you'll probably ask me what you can do to help.

And I wish I had an answer to tell you.

Actually, the answer I'd like to tell you, I am telling you by giving you this message and hoping you'll listen.

I think I need warmth from you, Mom—occasional kindness from pathetic, rational, lecturing, clueless Dad is not the same. But I think you can't offer it because all of us—including Dad—fight you, or because you no longer have any warmth to give.

Dad, you're not off the hook in this. I think you run interference between Mom and me and try to keep the peace. And then I think you escape when you go to work or play tennis with your buddies.

There is a good chance that neither of you will be able to understand me because I'm as different from you as you are from each other. But it might help if I saw you try.

And if I push you away, you might do well to stand firm and say, "We can't go away because as your parents we can't allow you to feel so alone in hell and we've got to do whatever we can to get you out." The dad of one of my friends actually sleeps outside her room on the floor. She hates it, but she feels safer.

I think I can live with the pain. I just can't live with feeling so alone. If I could feel less alone from the inside out, I could listen to what you and the world are telling me from the outside in.

Jack's father had sensed that things were bad for his son. But after he read this letter, he knew he had to take immediate action. I'm convinced that in doing so, he saved his son's life.

Like Jack, your loved one may be struggling with unbearable pain right now. And that person needs you to understand the depth of this pain. But he can't tell you. And you may be too afraid to ask.

Here's the solution: Open a line of communication with your own version of Jack's letter. Hand the article you've found to your loved one. Then gently say, "As soon as you have a chance, please read this and tell me what fits and what doesn't." And then walk away.

What will happen when you show your loved one this article? There's a chance it won't resonate much at all—that the person is actually strong at the core and is just going through a difficult stage. If so, he's likely to shrug and say, "Wow. That person is really messed up." Or you may even hear a puzzled, "Why did you give this to me?"

But there's also a chance that you'll open a floodgate. Your loved one may sob or even totally melt down.

If that happens, don't do anything but listen. And then say exactly what Jack asked his father to say: "I can't allow you to feel so alone in hell, and I will do whatever I can to get you out."

Then do it.

Usable insight ••••••••••••••••••••••••••

It's easier to bring up a painful subject than to wish, too late, that you had.

Action Steps

1. If you know or strongly suspect that someone you love is suicidal, call for help *now*.

2. If there is even a remote chance that your loved one is in deep despair or even thinking about suicide, decide—right now—that you will take action within a week. If possible, have other people who care about the person get on board with your plan.

3. Show the person your version of Jack's letter. And if you find that the person is indeed in hell, do whatever it takes to find a way out.

•••••••••••••••••••••••••••••••••••••• ▬▬▬▬

chapter 33

Woulda, Coulda, Shoulda

Preventing the Next Sandy Hook

THIS IS A dangerous chapter, and I'm hesitant to write it. But this topic is far too important to avoid.

Tragedies like Sandy Hook make it clear that we need to intervene in the lives of troubled young people before they become killers. We need to spot them early and listen to their pain.

Unfortunately, we're not doing that. Often, parents are too deep in denial to realize that their children are on the edge of the abyss. But even when parents do seek help for their children, these kids often just get what I call checklist therapy. A professional asks them a series of questions—"Do you experience thoughts of suicide?" "Do you feel depressed?"—and then writes out a prescription after a brief talk.

Some of these kids may indeed need prescriptions. But what all of them need is for someone to get inside their heads, where they're so very alone.

Here's what people need to realize: School shooters aren't born killers. Instead, many start out as outsiders. Over time, they become more and more disempowered. They feel denigrated, ignored, and invisible. As a result, they want to get even with the world—and then some.

The way to help these troubled people is to understand how they see the world and then get them to see it in a different way. But you can't do that with a checklist. You can only do it by talking. And this is a conversation that takes time, as my next story shows.

A few years ago, I saw a 22-year-old named Joe, whose mom wisely believed that he needed help to get out of the dark place he was in.

Joe came in reluctantly and sat down with his arms crossed, avoiding eye contact. Here's how our exchange went.

Me: Hello, Joe, my name is Dr. Goulston, and I get a sense that you didn't want to come today.

Joe (looking at me): Huh?

Me: You appear to be here against your will. So why did you come?

Joe: To get my mother off my back.

Me: Is she going to ask you how our meeting went?

Joe: Yeah.

Me: Any idea what you'll say?

Joe: No.

Me: How are we doing so far?

Joe: We haven't done anything yet.

Me: Well, you're looking at me—and you've stopped giving me the silent treatment.

Joe: What?

Me: Oops. I know. You're probably thinking, "Hey, man, don't push your luck."

Joe (derisively): You got it.

Me: When your mother called me to set this up, she told me that she was worried about you because you seemed to be in a very dark and negative place. Any idea what she meant by that?

Joe (sarcastically): I haven't got a clue.

Me: I have a feeling what you meant to say is, "I don't want to f#@&ing talk about it!" Is that close?

Joe (his interest piqued): Not a bad guess.

Me: And you don't want to f#@&ing talk about it because you don't think it will help. Is that close?

Joe: Bingo.

Me: While I'm visiting your mind, I'm also guessing that you're worried that if I knew some of the angry and destructive things you're thinking about, I might have to call in some people to intervene.

Joe (worried): What?

Me: Hey, don't sweat it. If I'm just guessing what's on your mind, without you telling me, I think you're still in the clear. Let's try another approach. I'm guessing that whatever destructive or even violent thoughts you're having, you have good reason to be thinking them. What I'd like to do is get to know you and really understand how you came to think those things, because I'm guessing that you haven't thought those things all your life. Now, are you willing to tell me the story of you?

Joe: Do you promise that you won't do anything when we get to where I'm at now?

Me: I really can't promise anything, especially if someone else is in danger. But what I will say, based on my experience, is that when I find out about how people came to be where they are now, I can nearly always help them find options that they didn't know they had. And to be honest, given our first few minutes together, I'm having a good feeling about that.

Joe: Are you going to put me on some stupid drug? Those things suck.

Me: I wasn't thinking of that. Why don't we just start with you telling me a little about who you are and how you got to where you are in your head and your life now?

Joe: Are you going to tell my mom anything?

Me: I wasn't planning on it. But you and I can come up with something you can tell her so we might be able to get her off your back. Would that be okay?

Joe: That's the first real positive thing I've heard, so now you've got my attention.

Me: Is that a green light to try what I've suggested?

Joe: Consider it a blinking red light.

Me: I'd prefer a blinking yellow light, but I'm game if you are.

Joe: Let's see how it goes.

Me: My, my, you're becoming talkative.

Joe: Don't push your luck.

Me (smiling)**:** Got it.

Over the next few weeks, Joe and I worked at uncovering the reasons he'd developed the negative and violent thoughts and feelings he was having. In our conversations, we explored his view of the world, which was that it was harsh and hostile. He described his fellow college students as "condescending a--holes." He said that his mom loved him, "But I know deep down she thinks I'm a loser." He said he'd never be able to get married because "girls are stuck up and they hate me."

Digging deeper, we got to the roots of Joe's negative worldview. We talked about his learning disabilities and the bullying he'd suffered in school. We talked about how a girl he'd loved deeply had recently dumped him coldly via email. We talked about his deeply repressed belief that he'd been to blame for his parents' breakup, and about the pain he felt when his father remarried, started a new family, and basically forgot about him.

I could see why Joe turned against the world and wanted to get back at it. But I could also tell that he didn't really want to hurt any-one—he just wanted to stop his own pain.

As we talked, I gently led him to see alternatives to his destructive way of thinking. Over time, he came to understand that he had nothing to do with his parents' splitting up. He also realized that his peers avoided him because he shut them out, not because they were jerks. And he recognized that being dumped by one girl didn't mean they all hated him.

Moreover, he learned that his mom didn't think he was a failure; instead, as she told him in one session, "I'm much more worried about you than disappointed. In fact, I think you're one of the bravest people I know. And I've always admired how hard you worked to overcome your learning disabilities. I feel like I'm the failure, because your father and I couldn't make a go of our marriage, and because I never realized how hard you had it in school, and I didn't do anything to stop it."

Joe's therapy wasn't easy, and all three of us—Joe, his mom, and I—had some tough days working through his issues. But all that work was worth it.

When Joe walked into my office, his mind was in a very scary place. But after several months of therapy, he was able to see the world in a new and better light. When we finally said good-bye, his life wasn't perfect, but it was well on the path to okay.

Why did I say this chapter is dangerous? Because conversing deeply like this with someone like Joe is risky. You need to think very deeply about the pros and cons. Before you even consider it, make sure you're emotionally resilient and can have this talk without letting the other person push your buttons, make you angry, and cause you to unwittingly escalate the conversation into a volatile situation.

Even if you are mentally prepared for this conversation, be aware that you're putting yourself at significant risk. Ideally, any talk like this involving a potentially violent person will be facilitated by a trained professional. After all, when you enter the world of troubled people like this, they may begin to see you as a savior— and when you can't save them from all their pain, they may turn on you (especially if they have borderline personality disorder). And that can put you in the crosshairs.

However, if you're the parent of a child who's in a dark place and is potentially homicidal, you're *already* in the crosshairs. Frequently, school shooters turn on their parents first. And even if they don't, those parents' lives are ruined. So whether or not you have this conversation, you're in danger.

Here's my recommendation: If you have any inkling that your child may be plotting the next Sandy Hook, try to find a therapist who's willing to use the approach I've recommended. First, visit the therapist yourself. Then include your child if possible, telling him you want help in becoming a better mom or dad.

If you can't find a good therapist, or if your child refuses to open up to a professional, then consider having this conversation yourself. Here are some things you can say when you talk with your child:

▶ "How do you see the world? It's important that I understand."

▶ "Tell me if there's anything I'm doing or saying that indicates that I don't understand how you see the world."

▶ "What's the most important good and bad stuff you've experienced? What do you feel and think as a result of those experiences?"

▶ "I can understand how you came to feel that way about the world. I'm just wondering if there's a different way to think about it."

If possible, rehearse this conversation with a therapist, even if your child refuses to see one. That way, the therapist can offer suggestions about guiding your child to find better solutions.

I can't promise you that a conversation like this can prevent a troubled child or adult from picking up a gun and wreaking havoc. But what I can say is that the worst feeling in the world after a tragedy like a school shooting is the feeling, "I should have done something." So if you're a parent, here's my advice: Do something.

Note: If you're a teacher, counselor, or coach who's worried about a particular child potentially becoming violent, I urge you to (1) discuss your concerns with the school principal and (2) encourage the child's mother or father to seek professional help from a therapist who's willing to provide the type of therapy I discuss in this chapter.

Usable insight •••••••••••••••••••••••••••••

The best antidote to woulda, coulda, shoulda but didn't is ask, listen, and listen some more.

Action Steps

1. Many parents of dangerous children or adults are in denial. If reading this chapter made you uncomfortable, ask yourself if your child's behavior upsets or even frightens you. Be honest, and think hard about the possible consequences of not being honest.

2. If your answer is yes, seek the help of a professional—not just a doctor who'll go through a checklist, but a therapist who will have an in-depth conversation with your child and help him develop a better, healthier worldview.

3. If you can't get your child to agree to therapy, or can't find a therapist who is willing to use this approach, have this conversation yourself.

••••••••••••••••••••••••••••••••••••••• ▬▬▬

Epilogue

I'M EXCITED and honored to share my ideas for talking to "crazy" with you. I've done my best to select approaches that are powerful and doable, not just in a psychiatrist's office but in the real world. Based on decades of experience, I know that these tools work for my patients, my business clients, and me.

But here's what I want to know: Are they working for you?

I hope you'll let me know. If you have a success story you'd like to share with me—or you want to vent if a strategy backfires—I'd love to hear from you. I'm on LinkedIn, Facebook, and Twitter, and you can reach me through my websites, markgoulston.com and goulstongroup.com, or my *Prison Letters with Dr. Mark Goulston* podcast. I've also started a campaign to provide "conversation catalysts" that will help you begin positive conversations with difficult people. (To learn more, go to http://patreon.com/drmarkgoulston.)

And one more thing:

Thank you.

One of my visions is that we can heal the world one conversation at a time. And every time you're brave enough to talk to crazy, you help make that vision come true.

Index

About the Author

Mark Goulston, MD, is a psychiatrist, consultant, business coach, and the author of the international bestsellers *Just Listen* and *Get Out of Your Own Way* as well as five other books. He is a former UCLA professor of psychiatry and FBI hostage negotiation trainer, and currently works as an executive coach and an adviser to CEOs and founders of Fortune 100 companies. He is the CEO and cofounder of the Goulston Group. His current and past clients include IBM, GE, Disney, Goldman Sachs, Deutsche Bank, Bank of America, Mattel, Xerox, Cisco, FedEx, Accenture, Goldman Sachs, ADP, Morgan Stanley, State Farm Insurance, Hyatt, the American Bar Association, Sodexo, UCLA, USC, the Office of the District Attorney of Los Angeles, and the FBI.

Named one of America's top psychiatrists by the Consumers' Research Council of America (2011, 2009, 2005, and 2004), Dr. Goulston is frequently quoted or featured in the *Wall Street Journal*, *Fortune*, and other publications, and on CNN, NPR, Fox News, and BBC-TV. He has contributed to the *Harvard Business Review* and numerous online publications, including *Business Insider*, *Fast Company*, the *Huffington Post*, and *Psychology Today*.

Dr. Goulston serves on the Board of Advisors for Health Corps and Brainrush and is the cofounder of the global community Heartfelt Leadership. He lives in Los Angeles.